THE POCKET GUIDE TO
THE 100 BEST GARDENS
IN IRELAND

Overleaf: Ballyrobert Cottage Garden

SHIRLEY LANIGAN

THE POCKET GUIDE TO
**THE 100 BEST GARDENS
IN IRELAND**

LIB
ERT
IES

First published in 2012 by
Liberties Press
7 Rathfarnham Road
Terenure
Dublin 6W
Tel: +353 (1) 405 5701
www.libertiespress.com
info@libertiespress.com

Trade enquiries to Gill & Macmillan
Distribution
Hume Avenue | Park West | Dublin 12
Tel: +353 (1) 500 9534 |
Fax: +353 (1) 500 9595
sales@gillmacmillan.ie

Distributed in the United States by
Dufour Editions | PO Box 7 | Chester
Springs | Pennsylvania | 19425

ISBN: 978-1-907593-47-5
2 4 6 8 10 9 7 5 3 1
A CIP record for this title is available
from the British Library.
Cover and Internal Design by
www.sinedesign.net
Printed by BZ Graf

*Previous: Lodge Park Walled
Garden and Steam Museum*

Introduction

When I wrote my first book of Irish gardens twelve years ago, the general plan was that it would not be a coffee table book. I wanted it to be a book the reader could put in a pocket and bring with them as they went visiting. Over-enthusiasm for the number of gardens open to visitors led to a book five centimetres thick and weighing in at not much under a kilo. It would need to be a reinforced pocket.

My second time out, the plan changed. I would only cover the top one hundred gardens on the island, chosen from over three hundred and fifty candidates. I would only write about the crème de la crème and this book would be a pocket book, portable and light. Enthusiasm stepped in again. There were so many beautiful pictures of the gardens to choose from. It was hard not to include them all because they each represented different aspects of the gardens.

Not surprisingly, it could hardly have been called a pocket book either. It would fit nicely into a medium-sized handbag. It could also be thrown into the back of the car. Still it failed the pocket test.

Finally, here is the pocket edition of the *100 Best Gardens in Ireland* and this time it will fit into a pocket. The text has been pared down and there are fewer pictures. It is now compact and portable.

I hope, in these shorter entries, that I have still managed to convey my enthusiasm for the gardens. These are places that I love dearly. In their own individual ways they are each glorious. Some are grand and formal. Some are small, intimate and informal. Some are architecturally impressive. Others are of horticultural importance. Some are of historic significance. But the one thing they all have in common is that they are glorious.

When I really fall for a place, I want so much to communicate that passion. I want the readers to want to visit in person the fine creations that are dotted so liberally around this island. If all came to all I would try to take them by the hand and conduct them in person to see these gardens. Doing that has been ruled out as somewhat impractical. This only leaves writing as enthusiastically as I can about my favourite gardens and obtaining good pictures of them to entice possible visitors to go and enjoy these exquisite places.

The hope is that this real pocket book will lure a few more people through those garden gates.

Shirley Lanigan
May 2012

Lissadell Gardens

Leinster

Burtown House

Altamont Gardens
Tullow

The history of Altamont stretches back many centuries. Monastic settlements, a nunnery and several families have lived and left their mark on this riverside site since before the sixteenth century. The house you see today is a dilapidated Georgian ghost that was built over the foundations of an older castle. The garden, however, is the creation of gardeners from the beginning of the twentieth century; first Fielding Lecky Watson and then his daughter, Corona North.

Since then, the existing gardens have been well cared for, restored and expanded. The expansion can be seen in the walled garden, where you will find the Corona North Commemorative Border made of plants with a special link to the garden.

Contact: The manager
Tel: (+353) 059 915 9444
e-mail: altamontgardens@opw.ie
www.heritageireland.ie
www.carlowgardentrail.com
For walled garden contact:
Robert Miller
Tel: (+353) 087 982 2135
e-mail: sales@altamontplants.com
Open: All year. Check web for seasonal hours. Supervised children welcome. Dogs on leads. **Special features:** Plant sales in walled garden. Guided tours. Picnic facilities. Partially wheelchair accessible. Toilets. Coach parking. Annual Snowdrop Week. Admission charge to groups only for guided tours. **Directions:** Leave Tullow on the N81 toward Bunclody. Turn left at the sign for Altamont.

The house and garden are reached by a short, wide avenue of beech trees under-planted with mountain ash or sorbus, and daffodils. To the garden side of the house there is a fish pool set into a slab-stone terrace studded with iris and angel's fishing rod or dierama. Arched yews straddle the wide path that runs downhill to the lake. In summer, roses teamed with dusty-pink double *Papavar somniferum* fill the beds on either side of the path, walled in by stretches of 150-year-old clipped box. In spring, sheetsof snowdrops, snowflakes, miniature irises and hellebores of all sorts fill these beds.

The pump-house walk leads past a range of rhododendrons down to the bund. This is a marl or clay wall that circles the lake, spiked with bright orange Welsh poppies, and creeping periwinkle or vinca.

During the Great Famine, one hundred men worked for two years to dig out this lake by hand. One hundred years later, Mrs North and her husband Garry would drain it, digging out a metre and a half of silt and over sixty fallen trees, before filling it again.

A path leads from the lake to the Ice Age glen and arboretum. The glen is home to over one hundred varieties of rhododendron and a number of venerable sessile oaks, including species of rhododendrons that came as seed from Frank Kingdom Ward's famous plant-hunting expeditions to the Himalayas. In the woods look for the One Hundred Steps that lead from the garden downhill to the River Slaney.

Kilgraney House Herb Garden
Borris Road, Bagenalstown

This is an interesting and singular garden. The house at Kilgraney was built in 1820, but when Bryan Leech and Martin Marley arrived to take over the old house with their elastic vision, they felt that the place could accommodate something more modern. They were right.

Contact: Bryan Leech
Tel: (+353) 059 977 5283
e-mail: info@kilgraneyhouse.com
www.kilgraneyhouse.com
Open: May to September, Thursday to Sunday and Bank Holidays 2pm-5pm. Unsuitable for children. No dogs.
Special features: Partially wheelchair accessible. Accommodation. Meals can be arranged. Art gallery. Herb oils from garden for sale. Car park not suitable for coaches.
Directions: Drive from Bagenalstown to Borris on the R705. The garden is signposted.

The house stands at the top of a tree-lined drive between fields of grazing cattle. The garden, entered by veering off to the side of the house, starts off behind a tall picket fence. This first small area is the vegetable and fruit garden.

Beyond this pretty but practical feature is the 'cloister' garden. This is so named as it is reminiscent of a cloister at the centre of a monastery. It even includes pews around the perimeter and a little central pond on which to contemplate. The whole structure is made of green

oak. This wood ages beautifully, turning a soft silver-grey as it weathers. The upright, silvering posts are draped in golden hop and vines, both plants that would have been grown in monasteries for brewing and wine making. Sitting in its pews, one overlooks the aromatic herb garden at yet another striking feature: a four-cornered arch of rusting steel spans.

On warm days the scent of lavender, box, mint and marjoram fill the air. Boxed-in beds of sage and rosemary compete with their own perfumes and on a sunny day the place is heady with herby smells.

At the bottom of this section of garden there is a little pond that is home to a small gaggle of Call ducks and other fancy fowl. The view from here out over a rolling patchwork of County Carlow fields and the huge horizon beyond is exceptional.

Beyond the herb garden they are developing a young fruit garden with a range of apples, pears, plums and quinces and a wonderful Celtic circle garden that promises to be worth investigating.

The genius of this garden is not in the inclusion of massive numbers of different species of plants, but in the creative use of a restricted palette. A bed full of nasturtium, or hollyhocks, dealt with by someone with a good eye is a thing of great charm.

Delta Sensory Gardens
Strawhall Estate

The Delta Sensory Garden on the edge of Carlow town is a feast of glorious gardening set in the middle of the most unlikely surroundings of an industrial estate on the outskirts of town.

Contact: Eileen Brophy
Tel: (+353) 059 914 3527
e-mail: info@deltacentre.org
www.deltacentre.org
Open: Monday to Friday 9am-5pm, Saturday/Sunday 11am-5.30pm. January to February closed weekends. Groups welcome by appointment.
Special features: Wheelchair accessible. Garden centre. Restaurant.
Directions: In Carlow town look for Cannery Road, close to the Athy road. The garden is signposted from here.

The gardens are attached to the Delta Garden Centre, a community enterprise running educational courses. The garden is in fact a whole series of gardens, set out around the centre. Some are contemporary, some are more traditional – but all were made as therapeutic gardens devoted to tantalising the five senses.

Each garden was created by a different talent, including designers and plant collectors Jimi Blake, Mary Reynolds, Elma Fenton, Rachel Doyle and Gordon Ledbetter, and these individual personalities are well in evidence in each of the gardens.

Mary Reynolds's garden, inspired by Yeats's poem 'The Stolen Child', is a strange, wild garden – a mix of native trees and shrubs, water and bog with a huge green sculpture at its centre. It is a lightly tended place teeming with wildlife.

For children, there is a giant games garden with monster-sized Jenga, chess, lawn darts and croquet. Quiet areas can be found through willow arches in little bowers at the ends of secret hazel walks, behind tall hedges, and in little sculpture gardens enclosed by tall yew walls.

There are classics like the rose garden, made up of standards, swags draped with climbers, ramblers and low growing carpet roses planted in regular patterns, all hemmed in by box walls.

There are also more modern ideas like the prairie garden, full of tall waving grasses and zinging splashes of flower.

The scents of flower and aromatic foliage are everywhere, from lavender and sage to roses and honeysuckle. You are encouraged to touch features from spouting, splurting and dripping water features, to rough and polished granite, limestone, wood, glass and metal sculptures.

This is a developing garden being run by the most enthusiastic and friendly staff and worth several visits at different times of the year, particularly for anyone new to gardening.

Airfield | Upper Kilmacud Road, Dundrum, Dublin 14

Airfield started life as a small farm and cottage dwelling in the 1830s. In 1860 and again in 1913 it was extended by the Overend family to make a larger house with a finer garden. The gardens went into decline in the 1950s, as Dublin and its suburbs encroached on the place, until eventually it became an island of neglected green in the city. In 1995 the Airfield Trust was set up with the aim of restoring it. Since then, the gardens have been continuously overhauled, reconstructed and greatly expanded.

Airfield's crowning glory is the walled garden, a flower-and-scent-filled place made of big herbaceous borders, a pond, rose and herb gardens, as well as trained fruit trees.

Hornbeam hedges were planted to divide the larger space into the smaller rooms that now make up the greater garden. It is designed to

Contact: The manager
Tel: (+353) 01 298 4301
e-mail: trust@airfield.ie / info@airfield.ie
www.airfield.ie
Open: Closed until 2013.
Special Features: Groups by appointment. Tours can be arranged. Supervised children welcome. Restaurant. Gift shop. Plant sales. Car and farm museums. Occasional market. Courses.
Directions: Travelling from Stillorgan on the Kilmacud Road Upper, Airfield is on the left and signposted.

be enjoyed from the terrace in front of the house when, in late spring and early summer, there are massive displays of tulips, grown in their hundreds through expanses of hardy geranium, alliums and thalictrum. Meanwhile, the scent from the huge flowering wisteria makes a grand accompaniment to lunch on the terrace later in the summer. From here, step down to inspect, at close quarters, the rose and pond gardens, the exotic herbaceous borders and trained fruit trees. Outside the walls, in one direction is Tot's Garden, a dry shade woodland feature, and in another, the Victorian greenhouse, the unusual dye and herb garden and wild flower meadows.

Hunt out the children's garden club outside the walled garden is where junior gardeners learn how to grow flowers and vegetables in a weekly club.

As a countryside visit set well within the city boundaries, Airfield is unique. The peace and quiet are remarkable and it is with something of a shock that one hits the noisy Kilmacud Road outside the gate.

Ardgillan Demesne
Balbriggan

The view from the top of the hill at the entrance to Ardgillan is a breath-catching one. Within the panoramic vista, there is a long sweep of lawn, a gigantic cedar of Lebanon, herbaceous plantings, regiments of clipped yews, terraced rose and flower beds, the house and beyond that the sea and the Mourne Mountains. While adults drink in all that, children will probably be tempted to roll down the hill.

Contact: Dominica McKevitt
Tel: (+353) 01 849 2212
e-mail: parks@fingalcoco.ie
www.fingalcoco.ie
Open: Daily: Winter 8am-5pm, Summer 8am-9pm. February to March 8am-6pm. April 8am-8pm. September 8am-8pm. October 8am – 7pm.
Special features: Garden museum. Castle. Tea room.
Directions: Travelling north on the M1, take the turn for Balrothery. The demesne is well signposted.

The Reverend Robert Taylor built the house at Ardgillan in 1738. Today it is in the care of Fingal County Council, which has restored the formal gardens using the 1865 Ordnance Survey maps for reference.

Pictures of Ardgillan always include the Victorian greenhouse, the centre-piece of the garden. This too was restored and it now houses a big vine and peach.

The huge walled garden is notable for its unusual free-standing walls built to create micro climates for the different plants which includes a special collection of Irish plants. The collection of Irish fruit trees, being trained along wires, is of particular interest to gardeners today, as growing native varieties is growing in popularity. The tiny greenhouses set at each corner of the walled garden might be dilapidated, but they are picturesque and hopefully they can be restored soon.

There are about 8km of paths through the woods, parkland and gardens. Three features not to be missed are the yew walk, the Lady's stairs and the ice house. The stairs is a quaint pedestrian footbridge which crosses the Balbriggan road and the Dublin-Belfast rail line, supposedly to allow ladies to cross to the sea for bathing. It is, as might be expected, haunted by one of them.

The Dillon Garden | 45 Sandford Road, Ranelagh, Dublin 6

It is hard to know where to start with the Dillon Garden. The word 'shrine' might hit the mark. This is a place of pilgrimage for gardeners the country over. Set in town in a not-too-huge space, it is a garden that fools the amateur into believing that they could imitate and replicate parts of it themselves.

Contact: Helen and Val Dillon
Tel: (+353) 01 497 1308
e-mail: info@dillongarden.com
Open: March, July and August, Every day 2pm-6pm / April, May, June, September, Sunday 2pm-6pm
Special features: Teas may be arranged for groups.
Directions: Signposted off Sandford Road by the church at the intersection between Sandford and Marlborough Roads.

Once past the cool birch garden at the front of the house, the notable features here are the hot and cool borders divided by the long central limestone-surrounded canal. The borders can be inspected from every angle and, like the best borders, they are different from every viewpoint and from one end of the season to the other.

Tucked in behind the cool border is the added surprise of a series of raised vegetable beds and big aluminium bins planted up with peas and scallions. Helen lines out the vegetables with the same care and style as the ornamentals.

It is almost impossible to see that the outer walls are made of stone, behind the massed climbers, shrubs, old tea roses, azara, potato vine and clematis.

Fine statuary, little paths tip-toeing in and around beds, the best garden flowers and 'trained-up' small trees are all features of the Dillon garden. The sunny back of the house is covered with a huge ceanothus. At the base of the wall there is a festival of troughs and pots exploding with bloom and scent.

If such a thing existed, I would recommend a season ticket for the Dillon garden.

The Duignan Garden
21 Library Road, Shankill

The Duignan garden is a remarkable place, a small-town garden that still manages to contain more beautifully grown unusual and rare plants than many larger gardens worth their salt. It is something of a horticultural Tardis.

Contact: Carmel Duignan
Tel: (+353) 01 282 4885
e-mail: cbduignan@eircom.net
Open: May to September, by appointment to groups and for occasional open days through the Dublin Garden Group.
Directions: On appointment.

Carmel Duignan has a talent and interest in propagation and experimentation and she takes full advantage of the sheltered aspect the garden enjoys to raise plants not often seen in Irish gardens. But for all its experimentation, this is no haphazard laboratory garden with all the nuts and bolts on show. The arrangements are perfect, and well thought-out combinations of colour and texture, height and shape abound.

The plot is a long rectangle, sloping up gradually with a central lawn dividing deep mixed borders on either side.

The colour mixes everywhere are strong and assured, so there will be a vivid yellow tansy with black ophiopogon grass, black dahlias with blood red Rosa 'Bengal Crimson' and red cotinus overhead. Carmel has a talent and interest in propagation and experimentation and she takes full advantage of the sheltered aspect the garden enjoys, to raise plants not often seen in Irish gardens.

Although she has a great interest in exotics, she is equally in love with plants that have Irish connections, and there are examples of this throughout the garden. Little paths pick their way between Clematis 'Glasnevin Dusk' with dark purple flowers, a fuchsia named after Christine Bamford, who bred fuschias in Wexford, and a Deutzia 'Alpine Magician', named by the botanist and horticultural taxonomist for the National Botanic Gardens, Charles Nelson.

It is a garden that one could wander through and enjoy hugely without a shred of horticultural knowledge. But for those with a more serious interest, it is a treasure trove of fabulous sights owned by a guide who can satisfy the curious with insight and information.

Farmleigh | The Phoenix Park, Dublin 7

Farmleigh, in a hidden corner of the Phoenix Park, was once the property of the Guinness family. It is now owned by the State and came as a stunning surprise to the public when it was first opened to visitors several years ago.

Contact: Sharon Doyle
Tel: (+353) 01 815 5900
e-mail: farmleighinfo@opw.ie
www.farmleigh.ie
Open: All year. Thursday to Sunday and bank holidays. Guided Tours of the house Wednesday to Sunday. There may be closures if required for Government business.
Directions: Drive up the main Chesterfield Avenue in the park in the direction of Castleknock. Near the Castleknock gates the garden is signposted to the left.

In the short time since it was unveiled, it has become one of the favourite national horticultural treasures, not only as a garden but as a venue for a whole range of garden activities, talks, demonstrations and expositions. Farmleigh is like a master class in Big House gardening.

The walled garden is of course the centrepiece of the garden. It boasts impressive flower and shrub borders, fine statuary set in among well designed walks and all sorts of special plants.

Lanning Roper, the American landscape architect, was responsible for the design. He had a great love of sculptural plants and his yew-backed borders here are perfection.

The greenhouse in here is something of a hub. In summer it is used for growing a number of different chillies and tomatoes; in winter it is hauled into service to mind oleander seedlings, as well as over-wintering semi-tender plants.

Outside, vegetables and fruit trees share the space with flowers and the ever-present deep tall yew hedges. There are two miles of yew hedges in this garden, cared for by Noel Ford, a hedging perfectionist.

On the subject of hedging, the Dutch garden is a marvel. This is one of very few examples of a topiary garden on the island. But this well-clipped feature would hold its own beside any other one might care to compare it with. The contrast between sharp shrubs and sunken beds of fluffy nepeta and tulips makes for quite a sight. And to get to it, the path runs through a cherry walk.

The grounds are extensive and take in lakeside walks and a boat house.

Marlay Demesne and Regency Walled Gardens | Grange Road, Rathfarnham

Set in the middle of great expanses of parkland, mature woods and walks, the Regency Walled Gardens at Marlay Park are something of a surprise. The rest of the demesne, while it is a great green oasis in the city, is essentially a park. But tucked behind a grove of ash, oak and yew, there is a quaint cottage like something from one of Grimm's tales. Inside is a tearoom, and through its trellis-surrounded back door there is a garden to knock the breath out of the unsuspecting, and even suspecting, visitor.

This is a restored garden of real merit. First of all, it is huge. Second, it is beautifully planted up. And lastly, it is minded with an amount of care and attention that is quite remarkable. I would almost dare someone to find a point worth criticising here.

Contact: Michael Church
Tel: (+353) 01 493 7372
e-mail: parks@dlrcoco.ie
Open: February to June, 10am-5pm/July to August 10am-8pm/September to October, 10am-5pm /November to January, 10am-4pm
No entrance fee. Supervised children welcome. No dogs.
Special features: Historic house. Craft shops. Partially wheelchair accessible. Coffee shop. Tennis courts, golf course, playing fields. **Directions:** Leave the M50 at Exit 13. Take the road signed to Rathfarnham, which leads to Grange Road. Marlay is accessed from the car park.

Of particular interest these days is the second walled garden, where the vegetable and cut-flower garden is sited. Widely spaced goblet-trained fruit trees stand over perfect circles of earth cut out of the lawn. In the vegetable beds, neat rows of chard contrast with billowing marjoram and parsley.

Past chive walls, we hit the raspberry and potato patches, medlar and current bushes, rows of loganberries, plums and pears.

Leaving this garden you notice the unusual garden sheds with curved walls. These are the old bothies, and today they house tools and pens for fancy fowl. The way out is under an ancient wisteria arch.

This glorious garden came about as a result of a long and painstaking restoration project. Using old maps and books from the early 1800s, the historic layouts of the long-gone garden were unearthed and restored. But the care lavished on the finished product is what impresses most.

Phoenix Park Walled Victorian Garden
I The Phoenix Park, Dublin 7

The Phoenix Park is one of the greatest jewels the country possesses as well as being one of the finest city parks in the world. Situated in the middle of the huge park, just beside Ashtown castle, the oldest building in the place, is the walled kitchen garden. This restored Victorian ornamental fruit and vegetable garden is a gem. Enter it from the central main entrance to catch the best first view of the chief feature – the central walk between the double borders backed by trained fruit trees.

Behind the trees you will find perfectly worked vegetable beds, like living textbooks on kitchen gardening. Next door, from mid-summer on, a little sunflower field becomes more and more dramatic and brash as the neighbouring pumpkin patch fills up with swelling monster veg.

Contact: Reception
Tel: (+353) 01 821 3021
e-mail: phoenixparkvisitorcentre@opw.ie
www.phoenixpark.ie.
Open: All year
Special features: Admission free. Wheelchair accessible. Restaurant. Growing demonstrations first Saturday of every month at 10.30am. Veg from the garden can be bought at weekends.
Directions: Situated in the Phoenix Park, close to the visitors centre near the Castleknock gates. Signposted.

The garden is worked by helpful and knowledgeable staff, happy to stop for a few minutes and answer questions. They also give regular demonstrations on growing throughout the summer season.

Don't miss a visit to the People's Garden down at the main entrance at Park Gate Street. This garden came about as part of a forward-thinking civic plan in the 1830s to create a 'Healthy People's Garden', complete with flower beds and drinking fountains of clean water for the citizens to enjoy.

On my most recent visit, as we drove past these, we spotted a huge gorilla sitting on top of a ten-metre pole inside the zoo fence, surveying his world, the fantastic Phoenix Park.

The National Botanic Gardens
Glasnevin, Dublin 9

The National Botanic Gardens in Dublin is one of the loveliest botanic gardens in the world. It is beautiful at all times of year, functional, well loved by Dubliners and visitors alike, a place of recreation and serious botanical research and conservation, a green lung in the city, a haven for wildlife and a tourist attraction of the first order.

Contact: Reception
Tel: (+353) 01 804 0300 / 01 857 0909
e-mail: botanicgardens@opw.ie
www.botanicgardens.ie
Open: Open: March to October: Monday-Friday 9am-5pm / Saturday-Sunday and Public holidays, 10am-6pm. Winter: Saturday-Sunday and public holidays 10am-4.30pm. No entrance fee. Car parking fee.
Special features: Wheelchair accessible. Restaurant. Book shop and visitor centre. Courses and lectures. Guided tours for a fee.
Directions: Situated on the north side of the city on Botanic Road.

Founded in 1795, the Botanic Gardens constitute Ireland's foremost botanical and horticultural institution. It played, and continues to play, a vital role in the conservation of rare, important and unusual plants.

The plant collections are a delight, arranged in geographical and scientific groupings in a landscaped setting on the banks of the River Tolka. The layout incorporates rock gardens, alpine yards, rose gardens, order beds, herb

and vegetable gardens, a pond, herbaceous and shrub borders, wall plants and an arboretum.

The four glasshouses include the Victoria house, built specially to house the giant Amazon water lilies beloved by generations of small children. Other houses contain succulents, palms, orchids, ferns and alpines. The curvilinear houses, built by Richard Turner in 1848 and with additional work carried out by himself and his son William twenty years later, are justly world-famous. They have been magnificently restored. The wonderful palm house has also been restored. These elegant houses, with their delicate cream paintwork, lacy iron veins and warm granite bases, are once again the pride of the wonderful Botanic Gardens.

There are so many sights to see at any time of the year throughout the garden. It might be a heavily laden Cornus kousa white with flowers or bracts, or the line of baby Wollemi pines, or my two favourites, the rockery and the great new walled organic kitchen garden. They grow over two hundred different crops in here, using a range of different organic methods to both feed and protect the plants from pests and diseases.

A whole range of people use the Botanic gardens for a whole range of reasons. This is rightly a much loved, much used treasure.

Primrose Hill
Lucan

Primrose Hill is one of the most charming gardens in the country. Attached to a fine Regency house attributed to the famous eighteenth-century architect James Gandon, it is a plantsman's garden, created over the past fifty years by the Hall family. That said, it has the look of a garden from another age; an old-fashioned, quirky, personal and colourful place, chock-full of plants, flowers and scents.

The impressive, hardworking Robin Hall tends this stuffed-to-capacity garden. His mother Cecily began work here in the 1950s when she took on the long-neglected site, turning it into a garden. The garden now has one of the largest collections of small flowering plants in the country and a famous collection of snowdrops, which can be seen during the spring.

Contact: Robin Hall
Tel: (+353) 01 628 0373
www.dublingardens.com
Open: February daily
2pm-6pm, June to end of July,
daily 2pm-6pm. Groups welcome
by appointment only. Supervised
children.
Special features: Plants for sale.
Directions: In Lucan village, turn
into Primrose Lane, opposite the
AIB Bank. The garden is at the
top of the lane. Buses must park
in village as they will not fit up
the drive.

Plants live cheek-by-jowl in this garden, between little stone paths and under a tall canopy of mature trees.

The sunny house wall is covered in an aged vine, intertwined with honeysuckle. The two gnarled trunks are like living scaffolding, architectural and lovely. Close by, in a shady spot, the fernery holds a sizable collection of native and exotic ferns.

I left leaving Robin a happy man, as the *Veratrum californicum*, given to him by the people at the Botanic Gardens eighteen years ago, had just flowered for the first time.

Royal Hospital Kilmainham

Military Road, Kilmainham, Dublin 8

Built by James Butler, the second Duke of Ormonde, in the 1680s, the Royal Hospital was modelled on Les Invalides, the retired soldier's hospital in Paris. The Royal Hospital in Kilmainham is considered to be Ireland's finest seventeenth-century building.

Contact: Mary Condon
Tel: (+353) 01 612 9900
e-mail: info@imma.ie
www.imma.ie
Open: All year (closed 25 and 26 December). No entrance fee.
Special features: Partially wheelchair accessible. Irish Museum of Modern Art. Bookshop. Restaurant. Guided tours can be arranged.
Directions: Travelling along St John's Road West by Heuston Station, turn left onto Military Road. The entrance is 200m along, on the right.

Lined along the north-facing front of the building, the restored garden stands below the hospital on a shelf of land looking out over the River Liffey and across to the Phoenix Park, which was also laid out by the Duke of Ormonde as a deer park.

Known as the Master's garden, it was an important feature of the hospital's design, when the governors declared that 'a garden should lie all open to the north side of the Hospital for the greater grace of the house'.

Its five acres are formal in fashion, in keeping with the French-style building and, as was also the style, it can be seen and studied in full from the main reception rooms. The layout involves four large squares, each sub-divided by horizontal avenues in a *patte d'oie* or goose-foot pattern.  Each path leads up to a focal point which will either be a piece of topiary or classical statuary. The planting is sparse and restrained and box hedges, lollipop-trained hollies, statues and soft-coloured golden gravel work together to create a cool, ordered, imposing garden.

The tea house, an unusual stone and red-brick folly, is the focal point. It is thought that this was originally built as a banqueting house, but it also housed the gardener and his family in the early twentieth century. The view from it through the garden provides a perfect picture of the hospital and its towering copper spire.

Outside the walls, the large hilly wild flower meadow is cut twice yearly, but otherwise left to nature. This area was the site of the old hospital graveyard. It leads up to the historic Bully's Acre, the oldest graveyard in Ireland.

The gardens at Kilmainham are both historically interesting as well as beautiful. Given that the National War Memorial Gardens are only a short walk away; a trip to both might make an interesting pair of military-related gardens. Add in a trip to all the gardens in the Phoenix Park across the river for a full-scale tour.

The Talbot Botanic Gardens, Malahide Demesne Dublin Road, Malahide

The castle at Malahide was lived in continuously by the Talbot family from the 1180s, when the lands were granted to Richard Talbot by the English Crown, until 1973, when the last of the family, Lord Milo de Talbot, died. He left the castle and lands to the Parks Department of Dublin County Council (the demesne is now managed by Fingal County Council).

Despite the lengthy history of the demesne, the gardens are young – they were largely created by Lord Milo between 1947 and 1973. He was a learned and enthusiastic gardener who set out to create a garden full of tender and less common plants, many of them from Tasmania, New Zealand and Australia.

The gardens are divided into the large pleasure garden and the walled garden. The pleasure garden,

Contact: Paul McDonnell
Tel: (+353) 01 890 5629
www.fingalcoco.ie **Walled garden open:** May to September, daily 2pm-5pm
Special features: Historic castle. Museum. Model railway. Tea room. Craft shops. Tours of garden on Wednesdays at 2pm, or by appointment at other times. To see auricula collection visit in April. Contact for opening details. Partially wheelchair accessible.
Directions: Driving from Fairview to Malahide, turn right at the sign for Malahide Castle. The entrance is on the left.

covering about nineteen acres, is made up of varied rides and paths, through almost five thousand species of tree.

The walled garden covers four acres and is divided into herbaceous and mixed beds, a spectacularly densely planted pond and the Australian garden, currently being developed in educational and formal arrangements. The greenhouses and alpine beds complete the walled garden. The Victorian greenhouse was donated to the garden by nuns in Blackrock in a fine example of recycling. The Haggard is a small area within the walled garden and in here one of the loveliest sights is the *Clematis nepalensis*.

One of the most notable things about Malahide is that they work almost completely without chemicals. Development and discovery are constant and ongoing here. Most recently, the uncovering of eight fireplaces along the wall in the Alpine garden gave rise to some interest. These were used to light fires that would create smoke, and thus deter frost from the tender plants in the little garden. Wonderful.

Burtown House
Ballytore, Athy

One of the notable features about the garden at Burtown House in Kildare is the fact that it is tended by three generations of one family: artist Lesley Fennell, her son and daughter-in-law, James and Joanna, and her mother, Wendy Walsh, Ireland's finest botanical artist.

Contact: Lesley Fennell
Tel: (+353) 059 862 3148 /
086 263 1485
www.burtownhouse.ie
Open: April to September. See website for annual details.
Special Features: Gallery and Artist's studios. Shop. Lunches or refreshment can be arranged. Partially wheelchair accessible. Coach parking. Supervised children.
Directions: Travelling south on the M9, leave at junction 3, then turn right onto the N78 signposted for Athy. Take the second turn to the left, signposted 'Irishtown'. Burtown House is the first gate on the left.

Burtown consists of several separate garden areas around the Georgian house, each worked by different family members. Lesley, however, is the chief gardener in charge of the big sunny borders around the walls of the house, the rock and woodland gardens running out from the buildings, the formal hedging and topiary areas, the orchards, water gardens and rose walks.

One of the loveliest of the gardens is attached to a converted stone outhouse and worked by

Wendy Walsh. It features a sunken stone slab patio.

Beyond the stone house is the oldest area in the garden – the big wood. This is set on an island surrounded by streams. It is a magical sort of place whose damp banks are full of trilliums, ferns, hostas and impressive *Cardiocrinum giganteum* under a canopy of tall beech trees, home to numerous bat, bird and owl boxes.

The walled kitchen garden close by is worked by James. This is dominated by a viewing tower in the middle that must be the best possible place for games of 'king of the castle'. Meanwhile, down at ground level, the business of producing purple sprouting broccoli, leeks, and rhubarb goes on.

Moving from the kitchen garden back toward the house, the path takes in more flower gardens and an almost secret, semi-wooded area starring a great spreading white-flowering cherry. With a flat head about ten metres across, it casts a gentle shade over large spreads of aconites, bluebells and lily-of-the-valley.

Before I left, Wendy showed me a tree that has a special place here: an Oregon maple or *Acer macrophyllum*. This is a baby of the famous maple in Front Square in Trinity College. Lesley's father found it on a rubbish tip in the college and transplanted it to an altogether finer life in a field below the house at Burtown.

Coolcarrigan House
Coolcarrigan, Coill Dubh, Naas

The Wilson Wright family has been gardening at Coolcarrigan for six generations. Today, the results of that work are seen in the classic Victorian garden, rockeries, lily pond, herbaceous borders, lawns, greenhouses and an impressive collection of shrubs and trees, which today stands at many thousands.

A visit begins with the more intimate area around the house. The chief attraction here is a classic border that impresses from early summer to late autumn.

Nearby is a handsome and well-stocked greenhouse that features a vine planted in 1900. Out on the lawn in front of this house there is a naturalistic pond cut straight into the turf. A few lilies decorate the water, but generally restraint has been shown and the main body of water remains clear to reflect the sky and trees. In the surrounding damp

Contact: Robert Wilson-Wright
Tel: (+353) 045 863 527 or 086 258 0439
e-mail: rww@coolcarrigan.ie
www.coolcarrigan.ie
Open: By appointment only. Supervised children welcome. Dogs on leads.
Special features: Lunches and tours by arrangement.
Directions: Drive from Clane to Prosperous and continue to the crossroads by the Dag Weld pub, from where Coolcarrigan is signed. Go through Coill Dubh. Pass the church. The garden is a short distance along on the left, marked by black gates.

lawns there are wild orchids in almost weed-like numbers. Naturalists will be delighted to see red squirrels, spotted fly-catchers and stoats.

The arboretum, for which the garden is justly well-known, has benefited from a long-time relationship between the family and the British plantsman Sir Harold Hillier, whose knowledge contributed hugely to the significance of the Coolcarrigan tree collection.

Heart, soul and finance continue to be poured into both the upkeep and advancement of this garden.

The Japanese Gardens and
St Fiachra's Garden | Kildare

In 1906 Colonel William Hall Walker of Tully, County Kildare, a man with a keen interest in Japanese gardens, brought a Japanese gardener, Tassa Eida, to Ireland to create a Japanese garden on the Kildare plains. Tassa worked with forty men for four years to develop the garden.

The miniature landscape is heavily laden with symbolism and meaning, based on man's journey through life from birth to death. Reading the symbolism is optional, however, and the place can be enjoyed simply as a garden full of mature shrubs, trees, gnarled topiary, waterside planting, and statuary. The garden is seen from a winding path that trails up, down, over and around rocky outcrops and past trees with carefully exposed root runs. A delicate old teahouse, the site of occasional tea-making ceremonies, sits high on one outcrop

Contact: Frieda O'Connell
Tel: (+353) 045 521 617 / 522 963
e-mail:
japanesegardens@eircom.net
www.irish-national-stud.ie
Open: February to 23 December, daily 9am-5pm. Guide dogs only.
Special features: Wheelchair accessible. Guided tours. Self-guided tours in fifteen languages. Café and shop.
Directions: Situated on the edge of Kildare town, signposted clearly off the N7.

and overlooks the different gardens. The little building is surrounded by bonsai, some of which have been in the garden since its creation in 1906.

The garden does not depend on flowers or plants that should be seen in the summer, so a trip off-season will be just as rewarding, and perhaps even more enjoyable, particularly in early autumn when the acers begin to colour.

Attached to the Japanese Garden is the larger St Fiachra's Garden. This is a woodland garden. Simplicity is again the keyword for the planting in this woodland and lake garden.

While you are at the Japanese Gardens you can also visit the Irish National Stud.

Lodge Park Walled Garden and Steam Museum | Straffan

T he walled garden at Lodge Park dates to the 1770s but it was restored in the 1940s and again in the 1980s. It is a charming, relaxed flower garden run by Sarah Guinness and talented gardener Patrick Ardill.

Contact: Mr &Mrs Robert Guinness
Tel: (+353) 01 627 3155 / 628 8412
e-mail: garden@steam-museum.ie
www.steam-museum.ie
Open: May to September by appointment / June to August, Wednesday to Sunday and bank holidays 2pm-6pm. Supervised children welcome. Horticultural and agricultural students free entry. **Special features:** Wheelchair accessible. Steam museum. Shop and tearoom, no entry fee.
Directions: Straffan is signposted from the Kill flyover on the M7, and from the Maynooth flyover on the N4. It is approximately 8km from both places. Follow 'Steam Museum' signs.

A visit begins at the top of the long rectangular garden, along a path that runs its length, with various rooms leading away from the path to the centre. The first picture is of a white garden full of pale, creamy flowers built around a stone well head and greenhouse with a little pond. On a warm day the sound of water and pale-coloured passion flowers make this corner feel quite exotic.

Meanwhile, the path continues on, under an iron 'spider web' arch covered by Rosa 'Francois Juranville' and on past a lean-to greenhouse on the south wall.

From early spring this small house is an Aladdin's cave full of cuttings and baby plants.

The double north-to-south borders are quite new. Backed by Sambucus niger 'Black Lace', they have been planted up with purple and blue irises, salvias, eupatorium, forget-me-nots and cornflowers. The font, from St Jude's Church nearby, stands in the middle of the wide grass path.

Beyond, one can see a sharply clipped beech hedge with an opening that invites investigation. But the path, bordered by huge, perfectly clipped yews and its own beckoning gate in the distance, keep one on the main trail, down past a line of good-looking shrubs.

Eventually, the path reaches the gateway and beyond it the herbaceous border and tennis court. In contrast to the darker double borders, this is all pinks and pale blues.

This is a truly romantic garden.

Kilfane Glen and Waterfall
Thomastown

Kilfane Glen was originally laid out by the Power family in the 1790s, a classic romantic garden covering a thirty-acre plot with a large woodland, deep in the middle of which is a glen with its own perfectly placed artificial waterfall, a cottage orné and hermit's grotto. The waterfall led into a meandering stream which ran through the wood, crossed at several points by rustic bridges.

But the original garden had become lost, swallowed up by choking *Rhododendron ponticum* and laurel. In the early 1990s, owners Susan and Nicholas Mosse painstakingly restored it, enlisting the help of late, famed designer Sybil Connolly to design the interior of the cottage, as well as redeveloping the garden in a manner faithful to the original planting.

Contact: Susan Mosse
Tel: (+353) 056 772 4558 / 772 7105
e-mail: susan@irishgardens.com
www.kilfane.com **Open:** See website for annual details. Groups of ten welcome all year. Supervised children welcome. No dogs.
Special features: Sculpture trail. Teas Wednesday, Friday and Sunday during open season. Picnic area. **Directions:** 3km off the Dublin–Waterford road (N9), signposted to the right 3.5km from Thomastown.

Apart from the old wood garden, several new gardens were created, including a blue orchard of crab apples grown in a circle and underplanted with grape hyacinths and bluebells. The orchard wall backs a blue bed of agapanthus, monkshood, delphinium and aubrieta. The formal pond looks down on the all-white moon garden.

Behind this garden there is a bamboo walk, a sort of hall of mirrors hidden in a laurel walk, and the vista, a view of Slievenamon through a clearing in the trees.

The most appealing features in Kilfane are the many paths that weave through the woods, going up- and downhill, running past rushing, gushing streams, under dark tunnels of trees and past little stepping stone features in openings in the woods.

Woodstock
Inistioge

Woodstock was the seat of the Tighes between 1745 and 1922, when it was burnt down and the garden, described as one of the finest in the country, began to disintegrate. In 1997, Kilkenny County Council and the Great Gardens of Ireland Restoration Programme began work to bring Woodstock back to something of its former glory.

A spectacular monkey puzzle avenue, made up of thirty-one pairs, thought to be the longest in Europe, was restored. New, young monkey puzzles were planted where older specimens had fallen. A decade on, they still look like tiny babies, sitting on tuffets of earth beside their huge relatives.

A second avenue of noble fir, almost half a kilometre long, running at an angle

Contact: Claire Murphy
Tel: (+353) 056 779 4033 / 775 8797 or John Delaney 087 854 9785
e-mail: woodstock@kilkennycoco.ie
www.woodstock.ie
Open: All year. October to March, 9am-4.30pm / April to September, 9am-8pm. Groups welcome. Car parking charge. Supervised children welcome. Dogs on leads. **Special Features:** Partially wheelchair accessible. Guided tours can be organised. Tearoom June to September. Playground. Buggy service to the walled garden during the summer. Contact for details.
Directions: Situated 2km west of the village, up a steep hill to the left of the two village churches.

40

from the monkey puzzles, was disentangled from a great thicket of rhododendron, laurel and bramble.

All over the pleasure grounds, clearances have revealed gardens not seen properly for nearly a century: the yew walk and kitchen gardens, only barely discernible until recently, were saved and restored. A box parterre was also replanted outside the walled garden. This leads up to the rebuilt Turner-designed greenhouse.

The walled garden is a real pleasure after so many years

of neglect. Today, its expansive beds of vegetables, mixed shrub and herbaceous beds, trained fruit and well maintained paths are a delight.

Although the once-famed collection of trees has sadly become depleted over the years due to storm damage and neglect, there are still massive wonders ranged about the grounds, including examples of *Sequoiadendron giganteum* (Wellingtonias), *Thuja plicata* 'Zebrina' and *Cryptomeria japonica*. Planting is ongoing, in part to make up for the lost trees.

Long woodland walks wind their way through the huge estate, leading in one case to a Gothic teahouse perched in the trees, with a panoramic view over the valley, woods and river below.

Gash Gardens | Castletown, Portlaoise

For years Gash was well known as the domain of Noel Keenan, the man who single-handedly developed this interesting garden. Today the garden continues to be worked by his daughter, Mary, herself a plant expert of note. Mary is developing and carrying the four-acre garden into the future, adding to its existing features and creating new ones.

The most memorable feature of the garden must be the moon house, a little cave set in the base of a large rockery at the entrance to the garden. It peeps out through a circular stone opening into a cascade of water coming from above. This is only one, albeit the most spectacular, of a number of water features at Gash. There are ponds, streams and rivulets criss-crossing the garden, travelling in all directions, dividing and linking different garden rooms, feeding the

Contact: Mary Keenan and Ross Doyle
Tel: (+353) 057 873 2247 / 087 272 8337
e-mail: gashgardens@eircom.net
Open: May to September, Monday to Saturday, 10am-5pm (Closed Sunday, except by appointment.) Groups by appointment. Not suitable for small children.
Special features: Teas can be arranged. Nursery.
Directions: 1km off the Dublin-Limerick N7 road at Castletown, signed.

roots of damp-loving plants and dictating the sort of plants that do best here.

The style is flowing and informal, taking in an easy mix of natural-looking rockeries, alpine beds, borders made up of herbaceous perennials, ponds and streams, mixed shrubs and flowers, laburnum walks, damp and shaded ferneries.

The garden was extended out into the countryside with the planting of a mixed maple walk along the bank of the River Nore. This stretches for a quarter of a mile along the water's edge. The simple desire to go for strolls by the river gave rise to this feature, one that will be there for centuries.

Heywood Garden
Ballinakill

Edwin Lutyens was an architect whose work with the great plantswoman Gertrude Jekyll is well known to garden lovers. He created a small number of gardens in Ireland with the help of Jekyll. Along with the National War Memorial Garden in Islandbridge in Dublin, the formal garden at Heywood ranks as the best known of his projects. Lutyens's garden at Heywood is a small but spectacular place, set in the middle of a greater demesne in the rolling Laois countryside and it is known and admired by garden visitors everywhere. Visiting today, it seems incongruously attached to a modern secondary school. The reason for this is that Heywood House, the property to which it was attached was destroyed by fire in the 1950s.

The main attraction of this garden is the sunken, circular, terraced garden with a central lily

Contact: The Manager
Tel: (+353) 057 873 3563
e-mail: heywoodgardens@opw.ie
www.heritageireland.ie
Open: All year daily, during daylight hours. No entrance fee. Supervised children welcome.
Special features: Partially wheelchair accessible. Guided tours by appointment (fee charged).
Directions: 7km southeast of Abbeyleix, off the R432 to Ballinakill (in the grounds of Heywood Community School).

pond surrounded by spitting lead turtles and a wonderfully over-sized fountain shaped like a huge champagne glass. Gertrude Jekyll designed the original planting and, while her plans have been lost, a study of her famous garden at Hestercombe in England gave the gardeners at Heywood the direction they needed. Nepeta, pink phlox, *Viola cornuta* 'Huntercombe Purple', peonies and Rosa 'Nathalie Nypels' fill the beds around the circular pond in two terraces, each backed by low walls and ledges.

A handsome summerhouse in grey, lichen-covered split limestone covered in jasmine overlooks the garden room.

But the Lutyens garden is only part of a larger garden at Heywood, and within its formal surroundings there are several small features that point to an older, different style of garden, which the years since have seen unearthed and restored; the discovery has added hugely to an already fine garden.

Heywood's most recent discovery down in the woods is an excellent example of late eighteenth-century romantic garden design. It was made up of trails or rides past a series of features: a sham castle, gothic follies peeping out from beyond woods and hills, orangeries, rustic and quaint stone bridges, artificial lakes, serpentine pools and streams. It is wonderful that this charming, wild and romantic garden has been saved from oblivion. The two gardens together make up one of the most satisfying garden visits I know.

Beaulieu House and Garden
Beaulieu, Drogheda

Beaulieu House was built in 1628 on the banks of the Boyne, refurbished between 1710 and 1720, and bears the distinction of being the first non-fortified house of its kind on the island.

Contact: Gabriel De Freitas or Malcolm Clark
Tel: (+353) 041 983 8557
e-mail: info@beaulieuhouse.ie
Open: May to September, Monday to Friday 11am-5pm / July to August, Saturday and Sunday 1pm-5pm. Not suitable for children.
Special features: Partially wheelchair accessible. Historic house.
Directions: The garden is on the right turn towards Baltray (R167) off the Drogheda to Termonfeckin road (R166), 2km from Termonfeckin.

The walled garden is set close by the house and is bordered by a mature wood. The Dutch artist Willem Van der Hagan, who painted an allegorical work on the ceiling of the drawing room, was also reputed to be a designer of walled gardens. If he designed it, that would date the garden to before 1732.

To get to the garden you take a path, bordered by golden yew and fuchsia, which passes a small temple-like building and a faded and fragile old greenhouse with a small grotto and fernery.

On stepping into the walled garden the visitor is greeted by a huge border on a wide ledge which looks down over the rest of the garden. Many of the plants in the border are old cottage varieties that have been grown here for generations. This is part of what makes the border so atmospheric and attractive.

At eight metres deep, this bed holds an enormous number of plants in creative and sometimes surprising combinations of leaf and flower.

Both the border and a knot garden sit on the raised ledge at the top of the garden. The level drops down to where the productive vegetable and fruit garden is sited. Down below, paths run under rose-covered arches and trellis with trained apple trees into the vegetable and working kitchen garden.

A sundial that seems hours out of synch as it trundles along at its own pace, stands head-high among the flowers. Losing time in Beaulieu seems a perfectly natural thing to do.

Killineer House and Garden
Killineer, Drogheda

On a hill looking south over Drogheda is the beautiful garden of Killineer. The house was built by a merchant from the town in the mid-1840s, when seventeen acres of grounds were laid out as a garden.

Contact: Charles Carroll
Tel: (+353) 041 983 8563
e-mail: info@killineer.ie
www.killineerhouse.ie
Open: Contact for dates and times.
Special features: Historic house. Partially wheelchair accessible.
Directions: Travelling north from Dublin on the M1, cross the suspension bridge over the Boyne. Take the first left signposted for Drogheda and Monasterboice. At the roundabout, take the exit for Drogheda. Go straight through the next roundabout, in the direction of Monasterboice. At the third roundabout turn left for Monasterboice. Continue for approximately 1km. The garden is on the right, marked by green gates.

I would bet that today Killineer enjoys the distinction of having the most extensive laurel lawn on the island. This is a remarkable-looking expanse of laurel grown as hip-high 'lawn' through which tall oak, beech and ash trees as well as more rarefied magnolia emerge and rise to produce a canopy overhead. Driving uphill toward the house, this is the first feature that greets you. The second is on the other side of the drive: the wide expanse of glass-smooth water of the man-made lake.

The house, standing at the top of the hill, looks sideways

toward the laurel lawn and straight down over sloped and stepped lawns to the bottom of the hill. A greater proportion of the garden at the bottom of the hill is light woodland and, in the woods, the damp ground is festooned with candelabra primulas. Charles Carroll has been busily encouraging their spread. One of the plants to seek out is the fourth biggest holly in the country. The strange knobbles on its trunk are indicators of its great age. A spongy bark path runs past this and under tunnels of rhododendron, among which there are red-leafed *R. arborea* and *R. sinogrande*. Everywhere, newly planted baby acers, magnolias and rare rhododendrons have been placed.

The walled garden, dating back to Regency times, is behind the house. Deep, varied, mixed borders run around the walls and a mix of flower and vegetable borders criss-cross through the one-and-a-quarter-acre space. It is a charming, bustling kitchen and flower garden.

The word 'substantial' best describes these gardens, with their sweeps of lawn, well trimmed hedges, and stands of trees and shrubs.

Bellefield House
Birr Road, Shinrone

Gardening expert Angela Jupe's latest garden at Bellefield House sits at the top of a drive between fields of grazing horses, culminating on a little meadow studded with scarlet tulips – a stylish start if ever there was one. A new orchard garden is being created to the side of the house, but the garden proper begins through the courtyard behind the house in the old walled garden.

Contact: Angela Jupe
Tel: (+353) 0505 47 766
e-mail: angelajupe@iol.ie
Open: By appointment.
Special features: Garden design service. Occasional plant sales.
Directions: 1km north of Shinrone on the N492.

When Angela arrived, to have called the walled garden a 'neglected mess' would have been kind. A 'mature walled wood' might have been more appropriate. A clearance was enthusiastically embarked upon.

Today the walled space is divided into two areas, on two different levels. The first section, set out on the lower ledge is home to the long greenhouse/sun room. This is where Angela grows some exotics, a vine and, in the summer, tomatoes. The area in front of it is formal, with a wide central gravel path and rill dividing two neat sections of lawn backed by shrub borders.

Stepping from here up to the main area, there are long, largely colour-coordinated mixed borders running in all directions. Down one wall there is a seventy-metre-long mixed border full of purple lupins and campanulas, plum-coloured poppies and blue nepeta. The original renegade trees are allowed to elbow in on the action at a few points. They contribute to the informal, individual style of the garden.

Down the middle of the garden is a pair of iris beds overlooked by the pièce de résistance – a rather wonderful, Indian-inspired summerhouse. This is a towering confection made from salvaged items Angela has acquired over the years. Within it there are old leaded windows that were salvaged from a convent, as well as the most wonderful copper cupola bought in a salvage yard in England. Angela thinks it came from India. The interior has been decorated using mosaic tiles. It sings of fun and whimsy and suits the flower-filled atmosphere in this seemingly effortlessly stylish garden.

Birr Castle Demesne
Rosse Row, Birr

The Parsons, Earls of Rosse, have been living in Birr since the 1620s. They are an unusual family. Unlike many stately home owners, whose studies were confined to the horse, they earned reputations for themselves as scientists, astronomers and philanthropists. In the nineteenth century they built 'Leviathan', then the largest telescope in the world. The family also boasts the invention of the steam turbine.

Meanwhile, they gardened their 150 acres. The grounds are filled with trees from all over the world, including arguably the most impressive *Cornus kousa* in the country. This collection of special trees is largely planted between great spreads of wild flower meadow, which adds immeasurably to the charm and unity of the grounds.

Inviting filigreed iron gates lure visitors from the park into the

Tel: (+353) 057 912 0336
e-mail: mail@birrcastle.com
www.birrcastle.com
Open: All year daily. See website for seasonal hours. Groups welcome. Supervised children welcome. Dogs on leads.
Special features: Telescope demonstrations during the summer. Gift shop. Museum. Gallery. Tearoom. Tours can be booked.
Directions: In the town of Birr, signposted.

formal walled garden. The smallest hint of what may be seen inside is gleaned when one spots the restored greenhouse in the distance at the end of a long path.

Also within the walls is a rose garden, a romantic little place, full of old French cultivars from the 1820s to the 1890s. There is also an intricate parterre, a 'cloister' made of hornbeam and the tallest box hedges in the world. The romantic air continues with the delphinium border.

Out in the open, in front of the castle look for the whirlpool spiral, made of lime trees. First planted in 1995, this spiral travels in ever-decreasing swirls, its shape reminiscent of a galaxy of stars.

Birr has many of the usual features expected in a great pleasure garden including, not a shell house, but a shell well, set deep in the woods. The mixed borders leading up to the castle and tucked in under the outer walls of mock fortifications are flowing and easy, herbaceous and informal.

Inside the castle walls, the high and low walks are equally lovely to wander beside, above and along the river. Waterfall Point looks down the spring-flowering bank to the gushing River Camcor below, and on towards a small suspension bridge, built in 1810, that leads across to groves of cornus, acer, willow, cherry and pine on the other side of the river.

Leaving the garden, one passes the castle gates, also built by Mary Rosse in 1850, with three ugly monsters to guard it, and a huge rose beside the portcullis.

Belvedere House and Garden
Tullamore Road, Mullingar

On hearing the history of Belvedere, one could be forgiven for thinking that they were listening to the plot of a particularly gruesome Gothic novel. This is the deeply unpleasant story of the three Rochford brothers, their three homes, Belvedere, Tudenham and Gaulstown, and their terrifying sibling rivalry. The brothers' lives seem to have been one long run of despicable carry-on, with stories of misfortunate wives locked up for decades, debauchery, duels, fights, vicious, quarrelsome feuds and casual cruelties.

The family history can still be seen today in the garden of Belvedere, in the bricks and mortar of the Jealous Wall. This well-named building is the largest Gothic folly on the island erected as a mock ruin by Lord Belvedere to obliterate the sight of his brother's larger home,

Tel: (+353) 044 934 9060
e-mail: info@belvedere-house.ie
www.belvedere-house.ie
Open: All year from 10am. See seasonal closing times on web. Children welcome. Dogs on leads.
Special features: Café. Garden centre. Gift shop. Events.
Directions: 5km from Mullingar on the N52.

Tudenham, built next door to Belvedere.

Several centuries on, the dilapidated gardens and deserted Georgian house were taken over by Westmeath County Council. They then underwent a serious programme of restoration and were opened to the public in 1999. Today, Belvedere is a centrepiece attraction and source of great pride in the county.

The seven-acre walled garden was built by a later owner, Charles Marley, in the nineteenth century. He and subsequent owners stocked it with a great variety of rare shrubs and trees.

The Himalayan garden is comprised of plants gathered on plant hunting expeditions. In the rose garden one will find the famous pink climbing rose named for the garden, *Rosa* 'Belvedere'. The greenhouses, meanwhile, are filled with the exotic perfumes and frilly blooms of an orchid collection.

The garden rounds off with the fruit, vegetable and herb garden. Some of the wall-trained fruit trees are particularly impressive specimens. The small pond and fountain pond full of Koi, collared by masses of flowers, probably shares joint place for prettiest sight in the garden, along with the view over the garden, with its maze of walks and paths, small hidden summerhouses and fairy gardens complete with ugly troll bridges.

Lough Ennell is itself as grand a body of water as such a house would require, with a wildflower meadow running up to the water's edge.

Tullynally Castle
Tullynally, Castlepollard

For anyone with an interest in trees, Tullynally will hold a special significance. It is the home of Thomas Pakenham, author and world-renowned tree expert. Travelling towards the castle, up the oak avenue, past elegant skeletons of fallen trees re-sprouting with new shoots, this feels exactly as the home of a tree enthusiast should, and serves to whet the appetite for such a magnificent place. Tullynally was built in the 1600s by the Pakenham family and they still live here.

The castle is the biggest castellated house in Ireland, sided by a yew hedge, cut like battlements that overlook the terraces and parkland.

The romantic landscape and garden beyond this date to the eighteenth century. Among its most beautiful features is the grotto. This curiosity is a little

Contact: Valerie and
Thomas Pakenham
Tel: (+353) 044 966 1159
e-mail:
tullynallycastle@eircom.net
www.tullynallycastle.com
Open: May to August 1pm 6pm,
weekends and bank holidays.
Groups at other times by
appointment. Supervised children
welcome. Dogs on leads.
Special features: Guided tours of
castle. Tearooms open weekends,
bank holidays or by appointment.
Plants for sale.
Directions: Situated 1.5km just
outside of Castlepollard on the
Granard Road R395 (signposted),
20km from Mullingar, 80km from
Dublin via M4 or N3.

stone bower perched up on a bank and tucked under a canopy of trees.

The kitchen garden covers a huge eight acres. It was built in the eighteenth century, when manpower was in no short supply. However, by 1840, when labour was still cheap, it was already being described as 'impossibly large for these times'.

Some of the huge area in the walled garden is today given over to a family of llamas that Valerie Pakenham told me are good grazers – or lawn mowers – and easily minded as well as being interesting to look at.

Past Queen Victoria's small summerhouse, the track leads to the 'bridge over the River Sham', well named because it is not a river at all but a serpentine lake masquerading as one. The summerhouse, too, falls into the same category: Queen Victoria never visited the garden, and this is a copy of one made for her elsewhere.

The grounds include American and Tibetan gardens, developed with plants native to both, and a recent development has been the addition of a new magnolia garden with thirty-six different species, set deep in the woods. In the meantime, a recently discovered rock wall full of ferns and moss has proved to be an exciting feature.

The adventure goes on, with Valerie in charge of maintenance and weeding as Thomas forges ahead, constantly planting new and unusual plants in the magical wood garden.

There are many remarkable trees here, but two are famous: a Champion Tree in the shape of a common beech that measures thirteen metres tall with a girth of seven metres, and the 'Squire's Walking Stick', an unusually tall, stick-straight oak. It was planted in the mid-1740s by a previous Thomas Pakenham.

Ballymore Garden
Ballymore Schoolhouse, Camolin

The garden around what was the old Ballymore schoolhouse is exceptionally good. It also comes as something of surprise, hiding as it does behind a tall laurel hedge on a country lane.

Contact: John and
Sylvia Mulcahy
Tel: (+353) 053 938 3179
e-mail: boo3@eircom.net
Open: By appointment and for annual open days. Contact for details.
Directions: In Camolin turn left after McDonald's Parkside Pub. Drive to a fork in the road and turn right. Drive uphill and take the left at two yield signs. The garden is 100m along and marked by a tall laurel hedge.

It would be fair to say that there is an overall Japanese theme and feel to Ballymore. In places the influence is overt and dominant: for instance there is a tea house, complete with rice-paper screen walls, perched on the edge of an islanded pond. Elsewhere, raked gravel expanses wash around massive boulders.

I first saw this garden in spring and it was full of flowering magnolias and acers with early unfurling colourful foliage, early alpine clematis, hellebores and snowflakes (*Leucojum vernum*). It was magical at that sparse time of year. As the year matures, so does the garden. One of the most memorable features is the laburnum walk and the little winding cobbled path under it leading up to a small red iron pig-gate in the distance. Later in the year roses, hydrangeas and clematis take over and splash the place with colour.

The final ingredient is sculpture. In every direction you see pieces of art set about, complimenting the plants and creating focal points. From a pair of overpowering Japanese guards to witty little metal birds and other creatures, there are works scattered everywhere. Even the shed is beautiful, clothed as it is in roses.

The Bay Garden
Camolin, Enniscorthy

Garden designers Frances and Iain MacDonald have spent the last two decades working together here in Wexford, creating and playing with what is both their garden and their shop window. This is a place built on patience and planning and it shows.

Contact: Frances and
Iain MacDonald
Tel: (+353) 053 938 3349
e-mail: thebaygarden@eircom.net
www.thebaygarden.com
Open: May to September, Sunday
2pm-5pm / June to August,
Friday and Sunday
2pm-5pm. Partially wheelchair
accessible. Guide dogs. Groups
welcome.
Special features: Plants for
sale. Garden talks and teas by
arrangement.
Directions: Situated on the N11,
just under 1km from Camolin (on
the Ferns side), opposite the turn
to Carnew.

Arriving at the front of the house, one is met by a welcoming little old-fashioned flower garden surrounded by tall stone walls and the front of the MacDonalds' double-fronted Georgian home. It could be straight out of a Jane Austin novel.

Exit, however reluctantly, by a side gate into a bigger and completely different place. Out here there is a large open garden with big colour-matched beds swept through by expanses of grass.

The trail leads from this big open area, and steps down to a

small, formal area. This is
a square divided by crossed
paths into four smaller
square beds, sharply colour
divided.

From here take the
trail through the Funereal
Forder, by way of the formal
yew garden, to the barn
garden. This is a sort of mad
spot where the meandering
trail winds between beds of
different grasses speckled
with flowers.

The wet garden is a new and developing feature. This was an expanse
of wet flood-plain that they planted up a few years ago. Building a
boardwalk to cross the damp ground over to a summerhouse was a great
design idea. Crossing it between crowds of astilbes, arums, ranunculus and
rodgersia feels like traversing a little jungle. Fern and container gardens
close to the house show that the McDonalds never cease conjuring up
new gardens. Their favourite recent creation, according to Frances, is the
small vegetable garden.

The growth here is phenomenal: look for the huge *Pinus montezumae*,
a giant at thirty years old, or the pretty *Cornus capitata* in the Japanese
area. There is now also a woodland garden, full of birches, Spanish
chestnut and beech.

'When everything else is gone the woods will be still here,' says
Frances.

Coolaught Gardens
Clonroche, Enniscorthy

Coolaught is something many help-strapped gardeners might envy – a family affair. Harry and Caroline Deacon and their family all work what is a whole array of gardens together.

Contact: Caroline and Harry Deacon
Tel: (+353) 053 924 4137 / 087 644 6882
e-mail: coolaughtgardens@eircom.net
Open: May to September, all week. Other times by appointment. No dogs.
Special Features: Plant nursery all year. Partially wheelchair accessible. Teas by arrangement.
Directions: On the N30, in the village of Clonroche turn at Greene's Supermarket. Drive 2.5k to the garden, which is well signposted.

In spring, the most memorable of these must be the crocus lawn to the front of the house. This small square garden is surrounded by big billowing roses with names as romantic as their scents – *Rosa* 'Ferdinand Pichard', *Rosa de rescht*, and *R.* 'Blanc de Double de Coubert' over sheets of *Geranium* 'Hocus Pocus' with crinodendron above and behind them.

This little gem of a garden leads out through a small gate into a laneway, which in turn leads to the first of a whole series of long borders running the length of the garden;

turning corners and leading into woodland gardens, past flower-draped arbours and into secret little sun rooms.

Open, sunny gardens full of perennials lead to gravelled herb gardens, and from there to the shade of flowering shrubs and fruit trees. The barn garden is particularly good. This is built around an old stone barn, the home of a big family of swallows in the summer. It is a purely romantic flower garden full of scent and flowers throughout the summer.

At the outer edge of the garden, there is a growing acre-and-a-half arboretum - a sort of trip around the world of trees.

John F. Kennedy Arboretum
New Ross

The John F. Kennedy Arboretum was set up in the late 1960s in memory of the Irish-American president, appropriately close to the old Kennedy homestead and it would seem a shame to visit one without a trip to the other. The arboretum is huge, covering 250 acres, and is laid out in blocks and groves of trees joined by wide paths, runs of grass and lakes. Alongside the profusion of specimen trees, there are two hundred forest plots. These scientific experiments were laid out to study how trees from different parts of the world grow as forests in Irish conditions.

Over 4,500 species and cultivars of tree and shrub from all the temperate regions of the world can be found growing here. The plants are arranged in a well-signed grid system.

Tel: (+353) 051 388 171
e-mail: jfkarboretum@opw.ie
www.heritageireland.ie
Open: May to August, daily 10am-8pm / April and September, daily 10am-6.30pm / October to March, daily 10am-5pm. Dogs on leads.
Special features: Exhibition centre. Seasonal tea room. Picnic area. Play area. Self-guiding trail. Guided tours may be booked April to September.
Directions: Travelling south on the R733 from New Ross, turn right 12km south of New Ross at the sign for the arboretum and the John F. Kennedy Homestead.

But it is also a pleasant walk. The walks are divided into two main circuits, one of broad-leaved trees and one of conifers.

Apart from the vast array of trees, there are displays of different hedging plants, varieties of shrubs, conifer beds, rockeries, lakeside and marginal plantings around the different water features. If you want to see a dozen differing species and varieties of cotoneaster, this is the place to visit and the same applies to sorbus, ceanothus, spirea, berberis and a great number of other plant families. Wild flower areas have been encouraged in a number of places.

The arboretum displays a wealth of trees and plants. It is worth taking a whole day to explore and appreciate it fully, taking in a walk to the viewing point. Up here, on top of the windy hill, the surrounding geography of Wexford, Waterford, Tipperary, Carlow, Wicklow and Kilkenny can be studied on a bright day, as well as the view out to sea to the Saltee islands.

Kilmokea Manor House and Garden
Great Island, Campile

Kilmokea is in the unusual situation of being sited on an historic site that was once an island in Waterford Harbour. In the early nineteenth century, land reclamation joined the little pocket of frost-free land to the mainland. Soon after, a pretty Georgian house was built on the site.

Contact: Mark and Emma Hewlett
Tel: (+353) 051 388 109
e-mail: kilmokea@eircom.net
www.kilmokea.com
Open: March to November, 10am-6pm. Supervised children welcome. Dogs on leads.
Special features: Partially wheelchair accessible. Art and crafts for sale. Teas and light lunches. Hotel. Guided tours by arrangement.
Directions: From New Ross take the R733, signposted for Campile and the JFK Arboretum. Pass the turn for the arboretum and continue for 1.5km. Turn right at the signpost for Great Island ESB and Kilmokea Garden. Drive 2.5km and take the left fork to the entrance.

Kilmokea is a romantic place, full of surprises. Plants and design, low walls, impressive tall semi-mazed hedges as well as elaborate topiary deliver year-round structure. I love the combination of formality and loose, easy planting.

The surprises are dotted around liberally. In one corner it will be an Italianate loggia with a formal pond. Chilean potato vine and lobster's claw clamber over the loggia in an unusual combination of colour and exotic-looking flowers.

Self-seeding is enthusiastically encouraged here. Everyone loves the sight of opportunistic blooms emerging from seemingly impossible situations, like the tops of walls. Occasionally a plant will park itself beside another surprisingly complementary plant, for which the gardener can, of course, take all credit.

The big kitchen garden, reached by way of a cathedral of bamboo, is another one of the great surprises. This is a busy, working but presentable vegetable garden, worked organically and built to wander through as much as to raid for food. Tall beds of sunflowers vie with the beans and peas. Low, undulating and wobbly box walls enclose flower beds, and lines of lettuce enjoy equal billing with dahlias and delphiniums.

From the house, the view down the bordered lawn directs the eye to a gate in a wall. Behind the gate there is a second, secluded garden with a fernery, beds of geraniums and paths that run under big camellias and rhododendrons, past wooden summerhouses.

Carry on through another gate and across a road to yet another garden. This is the real secret garden – a wild wood and 'horse pond' with a little boat moored picturesquely by the edge of the water.

Walkways and bridges have been set into the trees; Mrs Hewlett built all of these. They give the feeling of walking on gangways through a giant greenhouse.

Tombrick Garden | Tombrick, Ballycarney, Enniscorthy

Walter Kelly built the house at Tombrick in a small rectangular field on an extremely windy hill back in 1988. The following year he began a garden and today it gives visitors one of the most satisfying experiences to be found in what is one of the best gardening counties in the country.

Contact: Walter Kelly
Tel: (+353) 053 938 8863
Open: May to September, Friday to Sunday
2pm-6pm. Contact for annual dates. Other times by appointment. Guide dogs only.
Special features: Partially wheelchair accessible. Plants for sale.
Directions: Situated on the N80 between Bunclody and Enniscorthy, 1.3km north of Ballycarney Inn, signposted.

The garden to the front of the house is made up of lawn surrounded by borders, but not so dense that the sweep downhill to the River Barrow and the valley beyond cannot be seen. It is pretty but it does nothing to prepare you for what is in store. The real garden is to the side and rear of the house. It begins with a series of impressive ledged rockeries, and from there it moves out into woodland walks, sunny pond gardens, orchards and long serpentine paths through mixed borders filled with good and unusual plants.

Fancy fowl strut about the place, providing mobile entertainment and slug eradication along with a background of clucking and quacking. The fowl have their own pond, which of course doubles up as a water garden and home to collections of primulas, hostas and other damp-loving plants.

The paths sweep up against massed, billowing ground cover plants, well pruned small trees and invisibly supported tall herbaceous plants. The range and number of plants is stunning, as is the upkeep. How he manages to run a full farm and still find the time to work this garden, which looks like a full time job in itself, is a mystery. One could be forgiven for thinking that night work using a Davy lamp must be involved.

The gravel paths in particular give a sense of unity to the place, tying it together. They trail off in so many directions, lighting up dark wooded areas and making sunny bright spots even brighter. They are more impressive because they are so well minded, swept clean and clear of leaves.

Walter has a talent for combining plants that has to be seen coupled with a talent for presenting those plants impeccably.

June Blake's Garden
Tinode, Blessington

June Blake is, without doubt, one of the best plantswomen in Ireland. She has been selling fantastic plants from her nursery outside Blessington for years and her garden has been a favourite among visitors from all over. June's new garden is a rare treat, a modern garden that draws in the visitor and wraps them in flowers, welcoming yet stylish, and an example of virtuoso design and expert plantsmanship.

The garden is laid out in front of a house that similarly marries modern with cottage style. This is a gabled, granite Victorian cottage straight off the top of a chocolate box from one angle, but with a sharp modern extension of glass when viewed from another.

Generous beds of every conceivable perennial seem to vie with each other for attention. Gorgeous mixes and combinations

Contact: June Blake
Tel: (+353) 087 277 0399
e-mail: info@juneblake.ie
www.juneblake.ie
Open: April to September, Wednesday to Sunday 11am-5.30pm. Other times by appointment. Contact for exact annual dates.
Special features: Plant nursery. Part of the Dublin Garden Group. Refreshments. Guided tours.
Directions: Leave Blessington travelling towards Dublin on the N81. The garden is signposted on the left.

of flowers fill the place from early spring to the very end of the year. It is hard to know quite which direction to take first.

She has left happy accidents in place when they improve the look of the garden, such as the big arching cedar, which seems as though it might topple over a path. Items like this add more quirky structure to the perennial-heavy garden.

From secret paths set within and behind the borders to the obvious views up and down the paths and the panoramic view from on top of the hill, there is so much to drink in here. It is the sort of high-maintenance supermodel garden that looks as though it just tumbled out of bed, with tousled hair and looking naturally beautiful. You will not be able to do this at home.

Hunting Brook Gardens
Lamb Hill, Blessington

Jimi Blake has been a dynamic figure in Irish gardening for many years. In 2003, he moved home to Wicklow, and started a new garden from scratch in a field on the family farm. The resulting project has become one of the most highly regarded visits in the country, written up in a range of prestigious international gardening journals.

Contact: Jimi Blake
Tel: (+353) 01 458 3972 / 087 285 6601
e-mail: jimi@huntingbrook.com
www.huntingbrook.com
Open: See website for annual dates. Groups welcome.
Special features: Garden courses and lectures. Garden design and consultation.
Directions: Take the N81 out of Blessington in the direction of Dublin. 6km along, turn left and travel for 1km. The garden is on the left.

This is a large-scale garden, covering almost twenty acres, if you include the wood and stream after which the farm was named. But the garden proper covers about five acres.

Jimi's is such an individual's garden, not greatly influenced by anything other than his own interest in plants.

For a start, the house seems to stand in the middle of a large plantation of ligularias, inula, astrantia, coppiced eucalyptus and giant-leafed paulownias. One could have been dropped into a cabin in the middle of the jungle.

A little way off, the wood garden is at its very best in the spring. A network of paths edged with the branches of fallen trees give the wood an even more verdant and untamed look and with mature trees way overhead, the wood floor, dappled with light, is a sight for sore eyes.

Jimi Blake is experimenting constantly, changing what others would find perfect, adding in new features and different schemes. I suppose I should not try to describe it but just say: expect to be impressed.

Killruddery House and Gardens | Bray

Killruddery has been the home of the Brabazon family since 1618. The garden is unique – it is the only completely unchanged, classically French-designed, seventeenth-century garden on the island, partially designed by a student of the great André le Notre, designer of gardens to Louis XIV.

Contact: William Kinsella
Tel: (+353) 01 286 3405
e-mai: info@killruddery.com
www.killruddery.com
Open: April, weekends 9.30am-5pm / May to September, daily 9.30am-5pm. October, weekends only 9.30am-5pm. Otherwise groups by appointment. Supervised children.
Special features: Tearoom. Occasional rare plant sales. Guided tours of the gardens and house can be arranged. Events. Movie tours.
Directions: Take the M50s southbound onto the N11 then take the Bray/Greystones Exit and follow signs to Greystones.

Work started back in the 1600s and continued for centuries and, as a result, today the garden's great size, austere formal beauty and mature planting make it a singular place that leaves a lasting impression. It is a garden that can be visited (with permission) at any time of year as it is not a place that depends heavily on flowers but on strong lines, mature trees, monumental and large-scale plantations.

Killruddery's design is based on a number of large-scale features laid out along geometric lines, like an illustrated lecture on seventeenth-century garden design. The house stands on a wide terrace of granite overlooking twin canals that measure 187 metres and a wilderness or wood.

There is a beech-hedged pond, made up of two tall circles of beech, one inside the other like bracelets, with a circular walk in between.

A little way off there is another unusual feature: an amphitheatre, or sylvan theatre, with steps of grass-covered seats that rise up above a stage, backed by more tall beech hedging.

The area called 'the angles' is a series of maze-like walks between 4.5-metre-high hedges of hornbeam, lime and beech.

This quirky garden is overlooked by the house and recently restored orangerie (statue gallery), a beautiful glass structure built by Richard Turner in the 1800s.

From its windows you can see the ornamental dairy. This is a quaint, octagonal-shaped building with stained-glass windows, covered in roses and clematis. This was also part of a garden style that came from the continent in the late eighteenth century, when fine ladies would play at being milk maids and shepherdesses. Today it is used as a tearoom.

Kilmacurragh Botanic Gardens |
Kilbride

Named a national botanic garden in 2010, Kilmacurragh is probably the most exciting large garden on the island. Started in the 1850s on the foundations of an older garden, Kilmacurragh arboretum was always particularly famed for its conifers. Thomas Acton planted it between the years 1850 and 1908 in conjunction with David Moore and his son, Sir Frederick Moore, both of whom were curators at the National Botanic Gardens in Glasnevin, Dublin. Frederick Moore in particular recognised that it was possible, in places like Kilmacurragh, to successfully plant many exotic trees that had recently arrived in Ireland from plant-hunting expeditions around the world.

But the garden fell into decline in the twentieth century, and for many years it looked like the neglect

Contact: Seamus O'Brien
Tel: April onwards (+353) 404 48 844 / January to March 01 857 0909
e-mail: seamus.obrien@opw.ie
www.botanicgardens.ie
Open: November to February, 9am-4.30pm / February to October, 9am-6pm. No entrance fee. Dogs on leads.
Special features: Partially wheelchair accessible. Guided tours can be arranged.
Directions: Situated off the N11 at Rathdrum. Turn right at the Beehive Pub.

would never be repaired. Happily, Kil-macurragh is enjoying a renaissance and the current chapter of its history is going to read well. It is once again in the care of the National Botanic Gardens and under the expert eye and care of Seamus O'Brien. Under him, a programme of repair, restoration and development is galloping along and an extraordinary garden is being both uncovered and developed.

There are countless numbers of the biggest, tallest, widest, first-to-flower-in-the-northern-hemisphere, rarest and most impressive specimens found all over Kilmacurragh.

History is everywhere: the house is an unusual Dutch-style building, derelict yet still attractive. A wisteria over one of its side walls dates back to the 1830s. The remains of an older Dutch-style park garden can be seen in some of the vistas from the house, as well as a silver fir planted in the late 1700s.

Kilmacurragh Botanic Garden is gardened organically. Mown paths between the trees and a light hand make this garden feel as natural as William Robinson would have wanted. All over the gardens native hedges are being renewed, all propagated from plants grown in the locality.

Mount Usher Gardens
Ashford

Mount Usher is one of a small number of Irish gardens with an international reputation, one it has enjoyed since the late nineteenth century. Although it started life as a modest acre under potatoes in front of the holiday home of a Mr Edward Walpole in 1868, under the stewardship of his son, E. Horace Walpole, it rose to become one of the places that the famous Irish garden writer, William Robinson, championed as a perfect example of a fine garden. E. Horace improved it using the principles laid out by Robinson: in essence, to combine native and exotic plants in a naturalistic, seemingly artless way.

It has rightly been a favourite visit of garden lovers for generations. Today it covers twenty acres along the sheltered banks of the River Vartry, and is home

Contact: Philomena O'Dowd
Tel: (+353) 0404 40 205 /
0404 40 116
e-mail: info@mountushergardens.ie
www.mountushergardens.ie
Open: March to October, daily
10.30am-6pm. Supervised
children welcome.
Special features: Partially
wheelchair accessible. Tearoom.
Craft shops. Guided tours may
be arranged.
Directions: Situated in the village
of Ashford.

to five thousand different species of plants.

The shaded and sheltered winding paths make it is easy to get lost. Just roam freely, perhaps using the tree trail to discover the names of some of the many exceptional specimen trees here. The river runs like an artery through the garden, with weirs, bridges and waterfalls spread along its length; it is the soul of the place and the views along it in each direction have been carefully constructed to maximise its beauty.

'Layered' best describes the planting in Mount Usher. Graduated canopies made up of multi-coloured acers and magnolias, rhododendrons and eucryphias are breathtaking, particularly in autumn. Impressive trees and shrubs spread out every point, complementing each other in ways that look completely natural. Mount Usher holds National Collections of both eucryphia and nothofagus. The eucryphias, covered with white flowers at the end of the summer and into September, are one of the great glories and are worth a special visit.

Today, the man minding the garden is the enthusiastic Sean Heffernan. His has the all-important task of bringing the garden well into the next century, extending the fabulous colourful maple walk, repairing the waterways, maintaining the weirs and walls, and adding new features.

Patthana Garden
Kiltegan Village

Situated in Kiltegan village, Patthana is one of the best small secret gardens in the country. It is the garden of an artist – the painter TJ Maher – and it shows. Standing outside the old granite house, one gets no indication at all of the magical courtyard garden that lies behind the wooden gates.

Contact: TJ Maher and Simon Kirby
Tel: (+353) 086 194 4547
Open: August by appointment only. No Children. No dogs.
Directions: From the N81 in Baltinglass take the R747 for Hackettstown. The house is in the village, at the edge of the crossroads marked by an aubergine-coloured garage gate set into a granite wall.

This is a great example of fine organic, chemical-free gardening. There is more than a hint of the jungle about the abundance of foliage and even the cobbles you walk on seem to float on a green sea of mind-your-own-business.

There are so many distractions here. Each time one looks in a certain direction something un-noticed only a little while before becomes apparent.

Above the courtyard, there is a second garden. It is reached using steps made from stone water wheels as they pick their way up between prostrate, draping rosemary and hostas. The top garden is TJ's personal take on a country garden. Here, his reworking of the hackneyed island bed is well worth studying. Lightness of touch allows TJ to fit more beds and more plants into a small space, and the place never feels claustrophobic.

The top garden is surrounded by hedges of native holly, hawthorn, and euonymus. TJ cut windows in the hedge to frame a view of an old church spire in the distance.

Patthana is a garden I wish I had created.

Powerscourt Gardens |
Enniskerry

P owerscourt, set in the foothills of the Wicklow Mountains, is one of the great gardens of Europe, as well as one of the best-known and most visited gardens in the country. The lands here were given to the Wingfield family in 1609. In the eighteenth century, a grand mansion and formal grounds were commissioned by Sir Richard Wingfield, the third Viscount Powerscourt.

Tel: (+353) 01 204 6000
e-mail: carmel.byrne@
powerscourt.net
www.powerscourt.ie
Open: All year, daily
9.30am-5.30pm.
Closed 25 and 26 December.
Check web for winter times.
Special features: Children's play
area. Garden centre. Irish crafts
shop. Restaurant with terrace.
Multi-media exhibition on
Powerscourt's history.
Directions: Leave the N11 at the
exit signposted for Enniskerry.
The gates to Powerscourt are
a few hundred metres outside
the village on the road to
Roundwood.

The grounds at Powerscourt include forty-five acres of formal gardens, sweeping and stepped lawns, flower gardens, lengthy herbaceous borders, perfect clipped hedges, shrubs and woodland walks. Added to these there are walled gardens, statuary, follies, Japanese gardens, rambling trails, a monkey puzzle avenue, ornamental lakes and great variety of plants. There is also the largest pet cemetery in Europe and an arboretum.

For all its splendours, there is one feature that no one who has visited Powerscourt ever forgets, and that is the Italian garden. Designed by Daniel Robertson in the middle of the nineteenth century, what we see today took one hundred men twelve years to build. It was planned as a series of flamboyant terraces modelled on the Villa Butera near Palermo. The spectacle would look down over Triton's Lake, itself complete with a fountain modestly based on the waterworks in the Piazza Barberini in Rome.

But the work was cut short at a point when only the lake and the first terrace in Robertson's original design were complete. His benefactor, the sixth Viscount Powerscourt, died while on a Grand Tour and artefact-collecting trip in Italy. Years later, the work was continued by his son, in a modified way, yet the result is still lavish. It is an elaborate confection of wide sweeps of steps, pebble mosaics in elaborate patterns, statuary, wrought iron work, topiary and stunning views. Beyond the lake, there are mature woods and the perfectly placed Sugar Loaf Mountain in the distance.

The lake is just the most dramatic of the water features: everywhere throughout the formal gardens there are spouting, spraying, dripping and spluttering watery attractions.

Munster

Lisselan Estate Gardens

Bunratty Castle and Folk Park
Bunratty

Bunratty is something of a guilty pleasure. It is a place of bells-and-whistles exuberance. And while I can live without harps and medieval-themed banquets, the gardens are utterly charming – with icing on the

Tel: (+353) 061 360 788
e-mail: reservations@
shannonheritage.com
www.shannonheritage.com
Open: All year daily, except Good
Friday and 24-26 December. See
website for seasonal hours.
Special features: Gift shops and
restaurants. Medieval castle.
Partially wheelchair accessible.
Directions: Signed from the N18
travelling west from Limerick
City.

cake in the shape of farm animals, old fashioned farm and gardening implements and recreated historic dwelling houses with people in period costume carrying out tasks like making butter, bread and working little vegetable plots.

The reconstructed village, where the various gardens are located, stands behind and in the shadow of the fifteenth-century castle. There is a main street lined with old cottages, school houses, a doctor's house and little hovels. Beyond this there are recreated farmhouses from various points around the country and even a Georgian manor house. Each of these are accompanied by appropriate gardens. The prosperous landlord's impressive walled flower garden is the chief attraction, but the little vegetable plots, fenced in with old bedsteads, are interesting and instructive on the mend-and-make-do ways people had to operate.

The houses and gardens have been faithfully reconstructed and together they illustrate the different social layers in nineteenth-century Ireland. The doctor's house is draped with a massive sweep of Rosa 'Souvenir de Claudius de Donegal'. This particular garden is almost too pretty with its white picket fence enclosing runs of Jacobs's ladder, Welsh poppies, wallflowers, wisteria, poppies and geraniums, lavender and Lady's mantle. Meanwhile, at the other end of the scale, the smoke from damp turf fires clings to the clothes as one walks past the potato and cabbage patches in front of a small hovel.

The country house walled garden is laid out on a sunny hill from the top of which the whole garden can be seen along with view of the distant hills beyond the wall. This is a place of mixed shrub and flower beds, rose displays and wall climbers.

The best thing about Bunratty is that the size is such that, even on a busy summer Sunday, you can still have a peaceful walk around the gardens and there are seldom more than one or two others in each garden.

Caher Bridge Garden
Formoyle West, Fanore

With a background in ecology and countryside management, Carl Wright arrived here several years ago and took on a hazel and blackthorn-filled field around a derelict farm cottage. With these ingredients, in a landscape generally thought to be inhospitable to cultivation, he conjured up a plantsman's garden that sits well into its tuck of the landscape.

Contact: Carl Wright
Tel: (+353) 065 707 6225 / 086 080 2748
e-mail: caherbridgegarden@gmail.com
Open: All year by appointment only.
Special features: Wildlife talks.
Directions: Drive south on the coast road from Fanore. Turn off the road at Fanor Bridge over the Caher River. Pass the church on the right. The garden is 1.5km along on the right, just before the stone bridge.

As the stone was exposed, he studied the discoveries, and then harnessed it into the most appropriate features. So paths were put where the ground suggested it was amenable and steps were fashioned from existing stone formations that already looked like steps. This, of course, marries the garden further into its surroundings.

Because he had no soil to speak of, Carl used the many stones and boulders dug up to make raised beds, importing soil from the locality to fill these. Carl also uses pots and troughs to grow plants that would not otherwise thrive here.

The dominant feature to the side and front of the house is the pond. It is both unlined and fed from a stream, so it is just about natural. It certainly looks natural, colonized by native water plants including rare *Potamogeton lanceolatum*, hemlock, meadowsweet, bull rushes, yellow flag irises, comfrey and purple loosestrife.

The walls in this garden call for special admiration. They are all under ten years old and some are as young as two. But they were constructed with such craft that they look as though they might have been here forever.

Carl's is first and foremost a collector's garden and in the sunny area between house and pond there are 150 daylilies or *hemerocallis* and one hundred each of hostas, primulas and daffodils. All these are plants that we associate with soil, and if not good soil then at least plentiful. Carl brought every bit of soil in and then sieved it by hand. This is dedication above and beyond the call.

In the centre of the garden, the ash tree is a feature not to be missed. As he began to unearth the garden, this tree was discovered, bolt upright, growing between the old hazel trees, trying to get at the sun and, almost incredibly, growing over bare rock. Today, standing in a clearing, the big roots can be seen snaking over the boulders.

Vandeleur Walled Garden
Killimer Road, Kilrush

The Vandeleur Garden is possibly the most impressive community horticultural project on the island. In 1997, a group of Kilrush people took on the ruined walled garden of the old Vandeleur estate on the edge of their town, transforming it into an impressive garden, an employer of local people and a fine tourist amenity.

Tel: (+353) 065 905 1760
e-mail:
info@vandeleurwalledgarden.ie
www.vandeleurwalledgarden.ie
Open: April to September, Monday to Friday 10am-5pm, Saturday to Sunday and bank holidays 1pm-5pm. October to March, Monday to Friday 10am-4pm (closed bank holidays).
Special features: Café. Plants for sale. Gallery. Conference facilities. Wheelchair accessible.
Directions: Take the Killimer road out of Kilrush. Travel 1.5k and the garden is on the left.

Using the important Lawrence Collection photos with the other information unearthed from the Vandeleur archives, the team set to restoring the gardens. The work is now complete and the gardens are open to the public.

Today, in place of the many self-sown wild trees, large shrub borders encircle the walls. In the middle there are spreads of lawn, generous herbaceous borders, a small tree collection, fruit and vegetable gardens, a maze and a fruit walk, recently rebuilt glass houses, rockeries and gazebos.

On the sunny south-facing wall there are three-metre-tall exotic-looking echiums towering and flowering. Next to these, the informal display includes airy *Acacia baileyan*a 'Purpurea', rampant *hemerocallis* or daylilies, figs and *Melianthus major*.

The curved design of this sunny wall came about in an effort to maximise the length of warm wall space in order to accommodate the maximum number of sun-loving plants.

Outside the walls, the large courtyard dominated by a big bell tower has been restored and harnessed into useful life. Out here they planted a living willow for children to play in. There is also an old collection of puzzling farm machines, which should have even the most agriculturally knowledgeable people scratching their heads.

Beyond the walls, there are about fifty acres of woodland walks.

Annes Grove | Castletownroche, Mallow

Annes Grove has been one of the best-loved gardens on the island for a very long time, and rightly so. It is well known as one of the best Irish examples of a garden in the Robinsonian style. That style, championed by the nineteenth-century garden writer William Robinson, is the combination of native and exotic plants together in a naturalised fashion.

First stop on the trail is the walled garden, thought to have originally been an eighteenth-century orchard. A well-maintained run of curved box hedges, called 'ribbon beds' due to their 'twisted ribbon' design, leads to an unusual, primitive-looking, three-legged stone sundial. The box ribbons are permanent. Variety is injected from year to year in the inner sections,

Contact: Jane and Patrick Annesley
Tel: (+353) 022 26 145
e-mail: annesgrove@eircom.net
www.annesgrovegardens.com
Open: April to September. Check website for annual dates. Other times by appointment. Groups welcome. Supervised children welcome. Dogs on leads.
Special features: Accommodation. Partially wheelchair accessible.
Directions: Located 1.6km from Castletownroche, on the Fermoy–Mallow–Killarney road (N72). Signposted from the village.

which are planted up with different annuals. A little distance away there are two long borders.

Pergolas knotted with wisteria, honeysuckle and roses stretch out from these double borders, leading in one direction through a shaded, woody walk under cherry and eucryphia, to a lily pond. Beyond the water, the path ducks into the shade of a Victorian stone fernery, an arrangement of natural-looking stone ledges and mounds built to hold a collection of ferns.

Outside the walls, the wood and wild garden spreads in all directions. This too is a fabulous place but one in increasing need of care and intervention as it ages.

At the bottom of the descent, having ducked under magnolias and podocarpus dripping with little ferns and strings of moss, it feels as though you could have wandered onto a different continent. Only a few hundred metres back up the hill, the garden was cosy and familiar. Down here at the bottom of the slope, one could be in a rain forest. The River Awbeg snakes along the bottom of the valley, overhung with gunnera leaves over two metres across. It feels like pith helmets and machetes should be issued at the gate.

The path follows the course of the river, eventually emerging out of the jungle and into the open fields. The path wanders along, leading eventually to hydrangea rock, a gigantic open-air outcrop of stone rising way above the fields and covered in hydrangeas of every colour and shape. Another set of mossy, rough steps leads back into the woods to the top of the hill. I have never been able to follow the map provided, but it might be of some small use to those with a proper sense of direction. But getting lost is probably a necessary pleasure in Annes Grove.

Ballymaloe Cookery School Gardens
Shanagarry, Midleton

The old gardens at Ballymaloe have been in development and restoration since 1983, when the Allen family moved in. Today they are mature, varied and very beautiful. If there is one emphasis it is that, being attached to a cookery school, a number of the gardens are productive in one way or another.

Contact: Reception
Tel: (+353) 021 464 6785
e-mail: info@cookingisfun.ie
www.cookingisfun.ie
Open: June to September, daily 11am – 5.30pm. October to May, Monday to Saturday 11am-5.30pm. Supervised children welcome.
Special features: Garden shop. Cookery School. Groups can book meals in advance.
Directions: Signed from Castlemartyr on the Cork–Waterford road (N25).

The different gardens are not altogether attached to each other. I love the fact that there are courtyards and little groups of houses and buildings dotted about, again adding to a comfortable confusion. A visit generally feels like something of a treasure hunt. I would start at the stream garden beside the restaurant, where a gang of wirework ducks and geese, along with a few live versions, congregate by the water.

The well-known garden designer and writer, Jim Reynolds, created the fruit garden. It is not a large garden and its relatively compact dimensions mean it is well worth a visit by anyone with a modest-sized plot who dreams of an ornamental, productive garden.

From the fruit garden, a walk through a young beech wood leads to the *potager* – a French-style decorative vegetable garden. This is a confection of herringbone-patterned paths and über-smart symmetrical beds. This is not a place where you will find a messy gap: tidy parsnips, leeks and Florence fennel stand in measured lines. But marigolds and splashes of orange nasturtium soften the business-like look of the straight-laced vegetables.

Lydia's garden was named for Lydia Strangman, whose watercolours provided a reference for the Allens when they began the restoration work. This is a beech hedge-enclosed garden with herbaceous beds. In one corner, a tree house overlooks this and several of the other gardens.

The pond garden can be seen from the tree house. This small field of rose-clad cherry trees leads to a Grecian folly and a pond, the des res to a sizable population of tadpoles. There is an air of cool restraint here, with a simple palette of reflecting water, wildflower meadow and trees.

After such restraint, the punch that the big double border next-door packs is knock-out. These two beds, each measuring eighty metres in length and separated by a wide grass path, are memorable to say the least.

The borders culminate on the shell house. Its inner walls were decorated by shell artist Blott Kerr-Wilson. A mix of the usual and unusual shells makes up the fantastical geometric patterns.

Beside the shell house is a Celtic design-inspired maze of hornbeam, beech and yew. It is still young but small children will by now find it hard to work their way out.

Bantry House and Gardens
Bantry

antry House has been in the White family since the mid-1700s, when Richard White bought it from the Earl of Anglesey. In the 1940s it opened its gates to the curious and interested, becoming the first stately home in Ireland to do so. As a result, the Shelswell-Whites, as the family is now known, are well accustomed to welcoming visitors and they do it in an expert and informal way.

The garden was imaginatively restored about ten years ago after almost sixty years of neglect, and today it is one of the finer gardens in the country in one of the most extraordinary settings in the world. It is impossible not to be charmed by the place.

Bantry is quite unusual: handsome on a grand scale but

Contact: Sophie Shelswell-White
Tel: (+353) 027 50 047
e-mail: info@bantryhouse.com
www.bantryhouse.com
Open: March to October, daily 10am-6pm. Separate fee for house and garden. Children free.
Special features: Accommodation. Groups can book meals in advance. Gift shop. Spanish Armada exhibition centre. West Cork Music Festival venue.
Directions: Located on the N71 to Cork, 1km outside Bantry town, on the left.

also idiosyncratic and, despite its formality, a quirky sort of place. Bantry still has the feel of a home rather than a business enterprise.

The intricate Italian garden beside the house is such a perfect welcome to the garden. Within the box hedge boundary there is a fine circle of wisteria with knotty trunks that are every bit as good-looking as the dangling flowers and leaves.

The sunken flower garden to the side of the house is a busy mix of plants grown in circular beds.

The yew-and-box garden provides a smart contrast to this frothy flowery garden. From here it is possible to look down over the sloped wildflower meadow, cut through with a mown path. This could be a short-cut to the walled garden – today used for allotments.

For most visitors the glory of the garden is the stairway to the sky, which climbs up from the Italian garden. It is a monumental-scale staircase, cut into the steep hill above the house.

As well as looking so imposing from beneath, it delivers a view over the house, garden, Bantry Bay and the headland beyond. This is a view not to be missed. To sit and take in the panoramic sights from the top of the steps on a clear day is a privilege.

Beechwood

Templeisque, Glanmire

Ned and Liz Kirby are part of an enthusiastic band of fine Cork gardeners that leave the rest of us wondering if there is fertiliser in the water down there. They have opened their garden to the public for many years, changing and adapting it in exciting ways since its first appearance on the scene. It is a great garden to visit.

Contact: Ned and Liz Kirby
Tel: (+353) 021 488 4489 / 086 315 7096
e-mail:
info@beechwoodgarden.com
www.beechwoodgarden.com
Open: Summer months by appointment to groups only.
Special features: Refreshments can be booked.
Directions: From Cork go through Glanmire and on to Sallybrook. Turn left at sign for Sarsfield Court. Pass the hospital and go straight through the crossroads. After 0.5km turn left. The garden is on the left, a further 0.5km on.

Hidden from the road by a high beech hedge, it is firstly a plant-stuffed treat. A walk around should start on the garden side of that enclosing hedge. It shelters a sun-soaked bank of mixed shrubs knotted through with flowers, heathers and grasses.

Close by is a nicely matched collection of stone pots set into gravel. Chives, grasses and catmint grow easily from the gravel and variegated white and green sage spills out over the path. The sense is one of controlled chaos in soft, powdery colours. Giving good-looking plants the leeway to sprawl and spread for as long as they look pleasing is a talent seen everywhere here. Arched, plant-strewn steps lead from one garden to another. The framed views back and forward between the gardens show a good design eye working on every aspect of the place.

The house is hidden under blankets of ivy, cotoneaster, climbing lobster claw and golden yellow fremontodendron. The ground under all this is bright with a big run of variegated ground elder or *Aegopodium podagraria* 'Variegatum'. The Kirbys fenced it in, so they can enjoy the cream and green leaves without subjecting the rest of the garden to the threat of invasion.

Walking past a beech hedge cut into by a small gate, you catch a glimpse of a neighbouring field full of cows in a good example of borrowing nearby landscape and supporting cast. A low, banked bed along the other side of the gravel path spills over with mounds and hummocks of creeping hardy geraniums. Among these, more rarefied celmisia shows that this is another sun-trap.

So far so good, but follow your curiosity through another gateway in a tall hedge and the place changes radically. This is the wild garden, an exuberant and mad explosion of plants. Under the new design, even seeing the lie of the land is difficult: ponds, streams and waterfalls divide a dizzying maze of shrubs, exotic perennials and tall grasses on the hilly expanse. Much of the planting seems to grow straight out of beds of gravel or between mossy boulders. Quantities of stone make it feel like a bit of scorched Mediterranean earth in rural Cork. If the other side of the garden is manicured and well-mannered, this side is the wild child.

Cedar Lodge
Baneshane, Midleton

Described as a 'plantsman's garden', Cedar Lodge is unsurprisingly full to brimming with remarkable and interesting plants. Neil Williams is a man with a boundless wealth of knowledge, an understanding of plants and a photographic memory for plant names. A visit always feels like taking an advanced class in horticulture.

Contact: Neil and Sonia Williams
Tel: (+353) 021 461 3379 / 086 836 7303
e-mail: cedarlodgegarden@eircom.net
Open: April to August, by appointment to groups. Supervised children welcome.
Directions: Driving from Cork city on the N25, take the Midleton exit. After 200m turn right over the bridge. Take the first left at the roundabout and pass a line of caravans. After about 2-3km take a narrow right turn. The garden is on the right. From Youghal take the left exit off the N25 after the fly-over bridge for Midleton. Take the second exit from the roundabout and follow the above directions.

The garden covers almost two acres, divided into different areas that flow easily into each other and arranged in ways that show off his plant collection to best effect. Hard landscaping features are of course used, but the plants are the real stars here and all design is subservient to them. Everything is created to maximise the number of plants that can be shown to maximum advantage.

To the front of the garden, within the beech hedge boundary, there are a number of serpentine beds in a range of different sizes. All these beds are cut into a large expanse of lawn spread out in front of the house. They are arranged so that one will happily circle them again and again to fully study the mix of plants.

The whole front boundary is marked by a massive, deep border, running in a sweeping arc. This long, deep bed weaves in and out so that it is necessary to walk its length both ways in order to discover smaller treats like dactylorhizas and Chatham Island lilies. The bed turns a corner again and becomes a full-blown woodland garden before opening into an expansive area.

An elaborate figure-of-eight pond with a cascade, bog garden and raised rock bed is the central feature at the back of the house. The view of this from the terrace, through a well-placed window in a hedge, is particularly good but picking your way around it is the best way to see the little poppies, ferns and other plants it is home to.

An arched walk of roses and clematis runs the length of the garden and a walk under the tangles of *Clematis* 'Comtesse de Bouchaud', *Rosa* 'Étoile de Hollande' and wisteria is like a trip through a perfume shop.

On the other side of these scented climbers you can spy lines of onion, lettuce and beans between the tendrils and rustic poles. I like that the vegetables are both out in the open and yet partially disguised by the climbers and pergola. At the bottom of this walk, the paths branch off, leading between varied mixed borders full of perfectly maintained and unusual plants. When I think of order and perfection in a garden, this is the place I think of.

Coosheen | 15 Johnstown Park, Glounthaune

Coosheen is nothing short of a tour de force.

Hester and Patrick came to their third-of-an-acre site many years ago when it was given over to gooseberries and apples. They quickly began

Contact: Hester and Patrick Forde
Tel: (+353) 021 435 3855 /
086 865 4972
e-mail: hesterforde@gmail.com
www.hesterfordegarden.com
Open: May to September to groups by appointment.
Special features: Rare and special plants for sale.
Directions: In Glounthaune, with the church on left, travel towards the train station. Turn left after the station. Turn right across the slip road and the garden is second last on the left. Park on the slip road near the trees.

to experiment on the rock-hard plot that had, they discovered, once been the site of a quarry. The result of their labours is like the work of jewellers, a mixture of precision and elaborate display.

An obvious love of woodland plants can be seen everywhere: lovers of light shade carpet the ground under tree ferns, shrubs and small trees. The number of trees accommodated in this small garden without it feeling either too shaded or crowded is a testament to their great skill as designers.

Apart from small trees, if there is one unifying item in the place it is agapanthus. Their big and not-so-big royal blue, white, peacock and violet flowers seem to be everywhere.

Agapanthus aside, there are so many must-have plants here – from things like *Bessera elegans* which has strange square and hollow stems, to delicate little species *Gladiolus dalenii*. Contrasting-colour dahlias splash colours about the place liberally right through the summer up to autumn. There are always some roses in bloom, too.

The house is on a ledge and overlooks the sloped front garden, which is surrounded by a dense boundary of shrubs. The front garden is in the path of some whipping winds being battled creatively. In farming terms, there are no 'plainer cattle' here but it seems that the sheer number of special shrubs packed together, permit fine specimens of *Cornus controversa,* young blue cedars and Japanese acers to act as a shelter both to each other and to the inner garden.

The stepped area in front of the house is where the miniatures live; Hester has gathered quite a collection of perfect small specimens here. They include miniscule salvia, eucomis and geraniums. The little scree containers, with their tiny boulders, house fun-sized alpines – the sort of plants that might live around a doll's house. Baby hostas, miniature heucheras, leptospermums, minute cyclamen and geraniums are like Lilliputian delights, living the high life in well-presented tubs and troughs.

Hester could rightly be called a plant fashionista with an obvious love of the new and interesting. Be assured that she will be able to bring out some impossible-to-find treat and something, if not a number of things, you have never even heard of before. This is a garden that not only asks but demands multiple visits.

Dromboy

Carrignavar

S et in a rough hilly spot about two hundred metres above sea level in north Cork, Gertie and Maurice O'Donoghue's virtuoso garden is as hard to find as real treasures always are. Even arriving at the gates

Contact: Maurice and
Gertie O'Donoghue
Tel: (+353) 021 488 4555
e-mail: g.odonoghue@ucc.ie
Open: To groups by appointment and occasional annual open days. Contact for details.
Directions: At Rathduff on the main Cork-Mallow Rd (N20) take the Carrignavar exit. At the T-junction bear right, and take the next two left turns. The garden is the second entrance on the right.

and travelling up the long straight drive, there is little to declare this as the home of something special. Lined with well-clipped conifers, the drive is tidy and ordered but not especially indicative of the garden waiting to be seen. However, arriving at the top of the drive the magic becomes apparent.

A spread of perfect rolled, striped lawns sets the tone. The grass is edged in a way that almost defies nature. Meanwhile, the house straight ahead can barely be seen under blankets of climbers, creepers and general growth.

I could certainly live in their little hosta garden: this secluded corner is home to over 120 specimens and varieties, planted in big drifts around a little pond, under a grove of carved-out *Myrtus communis* and holly.

The contrast between this calm dark corner and some of the bright flower borders a little way off is almost startling.

Both O'Donoghues work the garden: Gertie is a plantswoman and Maurice has a talent for hard landscaping. Maurice also makes the fascinating sculptures placed around the garden. Together they have created a marvel of a place.

But for all its perfection, this is a personal garden and it is far from a predictable place. Many of the best vignettes include Maurice's sculptures. In one corner there might be an arch of ligustrum around a little statue. Nearby a miniscule stone pyramid, home to some lucky insects, will draw the eye. Elsewhere a gallery of stone heads almost stopped me in my tracks. They add a strange, extra dimension to the garden.

The surprises are around every corner, from secret pond gardens, sunny dry riverbed and scree gardens, to shaded mossy corners, formal flower beds and big bulging shrub borders.

Such an amalgamation of features and plant combinations so meticulously minded calls for the sort of study one visit alone will not allow. Ten visits might not even do it.

Fota Arboretum and Garden

Fota Island, Carrigtwohill

Fota was formerly known as 'Foatey', from the Irish fód te, which means 'warm turf' or 'warm sod'. This is an appropriate name for a garden that basks in the mild Cork climate and is blessed with a type of fertile brown earth so conducive to healthy, rapid plant growth.

The garden covers twenty-seven acres and is attached to the grand house built by the Smith-Barry family in the early nineteenth century. They took full advantage of the favourable climate. Working well into the twentieth century, they planted the finest trees and plants from all over the world here. The result was an arboretum of remarkable proportions and a range of pleasure gardens, including a fernery, an Italian garden, a walled garden and a lake. The house and land left the hands of the family and ended up in the care of the Fota

Contact: David O'Regan
Tel: (+353) 021 481 2728
www.heritageireland.ie
Open: Arboretum: April to October, Monday to Saturday 9am-6pm, Sunday 9am-6pm / November to March, Monday to Friday 9am-5pm, Sunday 9am-5pm.
Walled garden:
April to October, Monday to Friday and summer weekends. Contact for exact details. Car parking charge. Supervised children welcome. Dogs on leads.
Special features: Tearoom. Shop. Picnic area.
Directions: Take the Cobh exit off the N25 marked R624. The entrance is approximately 3km along.

Trust. The Trust has since restored the gardens and house magnificently.

The walled garden carries a collection of 160 varieties of Irish-bred daffodils, making it an unbeatable early spring feature.

Beyond the walled garden are the pleasure garden and the old Italian garden. Lined along the outside of the wall there are beds full of banana plants, verbena and hardy plumbago.

The paths lead out past plats of lawn that fill up with picnicking families and kissing couples in the summer. Pass the restored orangerie full of containerised citrus trees and make your way to the arboretum; advertising the location of it are two huge Canary Island date palms or Phoenix canariensis.

No trip should be made to Fota without a visit to the fernery, a natural-looking maze-like rock formation smothered in deep, velvety moss sprouting all sorts of ferns. Seeing a fernery on a dry day always feels wrong - visit them in or after rain. The leaves are at their best dripping water and in summer this place may even steam a little, giving an even more jungle-like feel to an already tropical place. Close by, and visible from the fernery, is the huge pond. This is almost as much lake as pond, a naturalistic expanse of water, with a scattering of lilies over its surface and wild flowers, gunnera, bamboo and grasses around the edge.

All this for a paltry €3 car park charge. Well done, Fota Trust.

Glebe Gardens and Gallery
The Glebe, Baltimore

Negotiating the tightrope between productive and ornamental gardens is tough, particularly when you are trying to produce enough to provide a restaurant with its fruit and veg. This is certainly no twee show garden. Jean grows a full range of fine produce, from vegetables and fruit to flowers and herbs, in a hard-worked five-and-a-half acre plot attached to her old house on the edge of Baltimore.

The flower garden is a beauty. Reached through the opening in one of the hedges, it is made up of double borders divided by grass paths. The mood is informal, with tall wigwams of sweet pea, lupins, amaranthus and euphorbia prettily twined around each other.

In the little courtyard garden, where the restaurant is, the smell of lemon verbena wafts around and

Contact: Jean and Peter Perry
Tel: (+353) 028 20 232
e-mail: glebegardens@gmail.com
www.glebegardens.com
Open: May to September, daily 10am-6pm. Groups by appointment. Supervised children welcome. Dogs on leads.
Special features: Restaurant. Produce for sale.
Directions: Approaching Baltimore on the N71, the garden is on the right-hand side opposite the 'Baltimore' signpost.

purple-flowered hyssop, rue, golden hops and echiums run wild.

I was taken by the ongoing experiments with outdoor varieties of tomatoes between purple-podded French beans, sweet corn, pumpkin, squash and 'Painted Lady' runner beans in the kitchen garden. This productive area is worked organically using the no-dig, raised-bed system. It is a hive of good gardening ideas and well worth studying.

Jean is an informative gardener and generous with her knowledge, so talks are regularly given at the garden by her and other speakers.

Poulnacurra Castle Jane Road, Glanmire

Mairead Harty's garden sings of her enthusiasm. Every corner is busy, worked and loved. This three-and-half-acre garden set around a fine Queen Anne house is, despite its setting, recently made.

Contact: Mrs Mairead Harty
Tel: (+353) 086 602 5791
Open: For charity days. See local press for annual dates. Otherwise by appointment.
Directions: Driving from Cork city to Glanmire, turn left at the traffic lights. The road forks just after that. Take the right fork onto Castle Jane Road.

For all its attractions, the most memorable features are the mirroring borders of catmint or nepeta, shell-pink and fuchsia-coloured roses that run up the centre of the garden.

Up at the top of the garden, running at a right angle to the mirror borders, is the millwheel walk. This is a long path made from about a dozen big millwheels. They were all unearthed from under decades of fallen leaves and humus when the garden was being made.

A new garden room close by comes upon the visitor out of the blue. In through a gate we catch

sight of a great explosion of flowers, roses and herbaceous perennials.

The individual garden rooms are punctuated by large lawns and divided by groves of acers, camellias and roses, all placed in combinations that block off and open up interesting views of other corners of the garden.

In stark contrast to the smart main garden, just across the drive there is a wild meadow garden, spiked with a mix of dog roses, weeping junipers, variegated azaras and embothriums, all planted in a more haphazard, natural-looking way.

Ilnacullin | Garinish Island, Glengarriff

Ilnacullin sits in the harbour of Glengarriff in Bantry Bay, an island with views out to sea and back to the mainland, reached by boat over a short stretch of water. It is without doubt the best situated garden in Ireland. Ride Brendan O'Sullivan's Harbour Queen out past basking seals draped over their warm rocks as you journey over the water.

Tel: (+353) 027 63 040
e-mail: garinishisland@opw.ie
www.heritageireland.ie
Open: 1 March to 31 October, Monday to Saturday, 10am-4.30pm, Sunday 1pm-5pm / April to June and Sep, Monday to Saturday 10am-6.30pm, Sunday 1pm-6.30pm / July to August, Monday to Saturday 9.30am-6.30pm, Sunday 11am-6.30pm.
Note: Last landing on the island is one hour before closing time. Supervised children welcome. Dogs on leads. Partially wheelchair accessible.
Directions: situated 1.5km off the coast from Glengarriff.

The thirty-seven-acre windswept, gorse-covered island was bought by Annan Bryce in 1910. He employed the famous English landscaper and architect Harold Peto to design a seven-storey house and garden for him on his island. The house was never built, and heaven knows what a building of such height would have looked like on the small rock, but today the garden stands as a reminder of that wildly optimistic plan.

The most famous feature on Ilnacullin is the Italian garden with its casita, or tea house, and pergola of golden Bath stone, inset with variously coloured marbles from prestigious Carrara to local Connemara stone.

Away from the Italian garden, the trail leads in several directions. One path with wide, rough stone steps leads to a Grecian temple on top of a hill with fine views over the sea. Up here all the formality of the lower garden is cast off – the impression is of tempered wild growth.

Trails through rare and unusual trees lead to the walled garden, a feature only partially open on my last two visits. Stretches of it are penned-off and not well tended – evidence of staff and money shortages.

Created by great gardeners, Illnacullin now needs another great gardener, to conserve and develop, and to stop it from deteriorating further.

Inish Beg Gardens
Baltimore

I nish Beg, set as it is on a secluded island near Skibbereen, feels like the sort of place where Agatha Christie could have had a wonderful time killing people off in a country house whodunit.

Contact: Paul and Georgiana Keane
Tel: (+353) 027 61031
e-mail: info@inishbeg.com
www.inishbeg.com
Open: All year by appointment, 10am-6pm. No dogs. Partially wheelchair accessible.
Special features: Accommodation.
Directions: Situated on the R595 approx 6km south of Skibbereen. Turn right just after the sign for 'Canon Goodman's Grave' and travel over the bridge to the island.

From the stone bridge over the water, the drive leads under some dramatic cedars of Lebanon onto a sunken avenue that rises up under lines of beech and oak. You feel dwarfed.

The house looks out over lawns bounded by unusual stone walls, groves of myrtles and magnolias and some very old white cherries. Standing in the rough field beyond all this is a poignant famine burial ground.

The main body of the garden is taken up with walks through and under woods, between groves of ferns and tree ferns, and alongside sunken, quirky-looking stone-lined

114

streams. One could be convinced that this is simply a case of nature untamed, wild and perfect. But it is a carefully tweaked, gently worked woodland garden of the best sort.

The jewel of Inish Beg is the unusual walled garden. This is a recent creation surrounded by low walls that come just to eye level. This is a good height as it means the garden can be seen and enjoyed from outside as well as inside and it also feels more open and sunny. Within the walls, wide paths break up big square beds full of decoratively arranged vegetables and flowers.

Ask to see the auricula theatre before you leave. Whether full of pots of auriculas in late spring, or empty during the rest of the year, this is a little beauty.

Kilravock Garden
Durrus

Phemie and Malcolm Rose have been working this garden for over twenty years, and gaining a reputation in Cork and beyond during that time. Walking through the lush garden today it is hard to tell that it was hard-won from a stony, boulder-laden site.

The place is full of unusual, rare and seldom-seen plants from all over the world and both of the Roses are avid collectors. There are thirty-two different restios alone here.

Another love affair with ferns led them to build a special fern house and a raised platform from which to enjoy a tree fern collection. Meanwhile, under the platform, the shade-loving ferns live beneath the fronds of their light-loving, taller relatives. As I visited Malcolm was busy, building another fern house; this one to house more tender specimens. It will have a warm,

Contact: Malcolm and Phemie Rose
Tel: (+353) 027 61 111 / 087 816 1526
e-mail: kilravock1@eircom.net
www.kilravockgardens.com
Open: During the West Cork Garden Trail and for charity days. See website for details. Otherwise by appointment only. No dogs. Groups welcome. Supervised children over 12 welcome.
Directions: 1.6km from Durrus on the Kilcrohane Road. The garden is on the right and signposted.

controlled environment with misting systems for the little plants. This is no ordinary garden.

There are hot areas with aeoniums, agave, eucomis and puya growing outside. The collection of cordylines includes an unusual prostrate species. Walking around the garden, it is clear that the Roses are keen on southern hemisphere plants, and Dunmanus Bay allows them to indulge their tastes fairly comprehensively.

West Cork's frost-free climate is an advantage that midlanders envy. It is hampered somewhat by salt winds, so a tall hedge shelters the bottom part of the garden, protecting it from the spray that whips up from the bay. The hedge is not so tall that it prevents a good view of the water however. The two-acre garden is ice-cream-cone-shaped, with the narrow end reached through a tunnel of white wisteria, golden hops, including an unusual clematis with small, fat and spongy purple flowers. Finally, there is the Mediterranean tower. Yes, a Mediterranean tower.

Lakemount
Barnavara Hill, Glanmire

Lakemount was started over half a century ago by Brian Cross's mother on the site of a chicken and fruit farm. He joined her the age of eight, when he began to grow Sweet William seeds. Today, Lakemount is famous around the horticultural world – a sophisticated garden, beautiful, well groomed and in a constant state of development.

Contact: Brian and Rose Cross
Tel: (+353) 086 811 0241
e-mail: crosscork@gmail.com
www.irelandsgardens.com /
www.lakemountgarden.com
Open: By appointment.
Not suitable for children.
Directions: Drive from Cork on the R639 to Glanmire to Riverstown Cross. Turn left at the lights and go up Barnavara Hill. The garden is on the left past the 50km sign and marked by a stone wall and black gate.

The garden is cleverly divided into intimate, secluded rooms or compartments, each with a particular mood. In one, canna lilies form a two-and-a-half-metre-high wall over beds full of multi-shaded pink penstemon. Brian mixes colour like a master painter, and here rich purple *Verbena bonariensis* and reddish-black chocolate cosmos is only one luscious colour combination.

Lakemount garden covers two acres but the shape and style is such that it seems even bigger, and walking back and forward one finds oneself revisiting rooms already seen from other paths and angles. Labyrinthine trails wander in all directions, dividing rooms and leading from one to another with steps up and down and gates leading here and there. There are gates at every turn: low, wrought-iron, wooden and picket fence gates lead through arches of rose and honeysuckle. Little summerhouses smothered in clematis sit secluded in quiet corners.

The greenhouse has been so densely covered in creepers that the building looks like it was constructed from leaves, flowers and glass.

Brian Cross is one of the few gardeners happy for his garden to be inspected at times other than May and June, declaring it to be at its best in the autumn.

Lisselan Estate Gardens
Clonakilty

The gardens at Lisselan are set in a valley beside the River Argideen. Covering around twenty acres, they were laid out by the Bence-Jones family in the last century following the principles of William Robinson, the famous Irish garden designer and writer. They must be among the most romantic, peaceful and handsome gardens on the island, a perfect combination of water, flowers, wildlife, fine trees, tranquillity and taste.

The first view most visitors get of the garden is the rock garden at the foot of the house. The building is reminiscent of a French château, all turrets and gables draped in Virginia creeper. It stands on a cartoon-like precipice looking down on the garden. That precipice is laid out as a rock garden, steeply sloped from the base of the building down to the river valley floor. It is a bold,

Contact: Mark Coombes
Tel: (+353) 023 883 3249
e-mail: info@lisselan.com
www.lisselan.com
Open: All year daily, 8am-Dusk. Groups must book. Supervised children welcome. No dogs.
Special features: Guided tours. Partially wheelchair accessible. Teas can be booked. Golf course.
Directions: Located 3km from Clonakilty town, on the N71 travelling towards Cork city.

memorable feature. For visitors with the footing of mountain goats it is possible to climb up the rockery and through it. The rockery is one of the most beautiful features in the county and worth a major detour in its own right.

Off to the west of the house is an impressive shrubbery with mature pines overhead and acacia, myrtle, robinia and vivid-coloured rhododendrons beneath. A meandering walk called the ladies' mile leads through this, along the river and though the rhododendron woods. A long, rough-paved set of steps covered by arched trees and edged with dahlias and other flowers leads down to this river walk.

The most recent development at Lisselan is the fuchsia garden. This has been developed in the old walled garden, at the far reaches of the main river walk.

Derreen
Lauragh, Killarney

D erreen is a singular garden, a place of such charm and beauty that it lodges in the memory in a way that much showier gardens usually don't. A completely man-made garden, it nevertheless has an air of untamed nature about it. When lists of quintessentially Irish gardens are made, it is always at the top.

Contact: Jacky Ward, Head Gardener
Tel: (+353) 064 668 3588
www.derreengarden.com
Open: All year daily, 10am-6pm. Supervised children welcome. Dogs on leads.
Special features: Teas can be booked in advance. Guided tours.
Directions: Derreen is 24km from Kenmare on the R571 travelling toward Castletownbere. Signposted.

In the 1600s the lands at Derreen were among the massive tracts owned by the Cromwellian William Petty, the man who carried out the Down Survey. (This was the first great land survey of the south and west of Ireland, carried out in order to redistribute lands confiscated from Irish landowners.) He was paid for his work with 270,000 acres in Kerry, and the lands moved through his family and a series of tenants until the 1850s, when the Lansdowne family, as they were known by then, began to take an interest in the property at Derreen and its grounds.

Today, Derreen is a large woodland garden, created through the improvements carried out by the fifth Marquess of Lansdowne in the 1870s.

The garden visit begins close to the house by the big rock. This is a massive, flat, smooth outcrop of stone, known since ancient times as a meeting place.

Between the sheltering trees are the tree ferns or *Dicksonia antarctica*, for which Derreen has become famous. They grow in such numbers and sizes that they only serve to highlight the difficulty of growing even fairly scrawny specimens elsewhere in the country.

One of the best areas in the garden is the Knockatee seat, perched to take in a view over the woods to Knockatee Hill. A knobbly path picks its way up towards it between rocks, trees and ferns.

The magic of Derreen lies in its being so wild, and huge barriers of bamboo cross the path. But the wildness is contrived; the garden has been tended for many years by Jacky Ward. We have to remind ourselves that if it was actually wild it would disappear under native weeds. Impression is everything. A more romantic soul might be moved to lie down on the moss and commune with nature. Appropriately, the method of payment here is through a rarely seen honesty box.

Derrynane National Historic Park
Caherdaniel

Memories of trips to Derrynane years ago involve sitting on the grass in front of the slate-sided house for picnics and guided tours of 'The Liberator' Daniel O'Connell's home. Today a trip to Derrynane conjures up pictures of Wellington-clad expeditions through a fascinating and growing plant collection in this expanding, experimental wild garden.

A number of years ago the garden was allied to the Edinburgh Botanic Gardens and as such was chosen to trial a whole array of seeds and plants collected in far-flung places.

Entrance to this laboratory garden is through a stone arch under the drive, draped with variegated clerodendron and mulberry. Once inside, instead of finding sterile lab

Contact: James O'Shea
Tel: (+353) 066 947 5387
e-mail: derrynanehouse@opw.ie
Open: All year during daylight hours. Free admission. Supervised children welcome. Dogs on leads.
Special features: Café, Historic house. Partially wheelchair accessible.
Directions: 3.5km from Caherdaniel, off the N70. Signposted.

conditions and neat rows, the plants are arranged in ways that they might look in the wild.

Huge rainfall, the lush growth, sheltering neighbours and soft climate bestow the conditions that allow plants to grow with great vigour. Plants from Chile, Argentina, Brazil, Australia and New Zealand, usually seen snug and pampered in greenhouses, are all growing outside quite happily.

Much of the garden is taken up with expanses of sunny lawn studded with these wild island beds and protruding rocks. Meanwhile, groves of tall oak and English elm tower so far overhead that they cast very little shadow on the gardens below. Shaded spots like the fern and rock garden link the more open areas to unusual features, such as the field of tree ferns. The experiment at Derrynane is in its infancy and it will be a great pleasure to watch it develop in years to come.

Hotel Dunloe Castle Gardens
Beaufort, Killarney

The Hotel Dunloe Castle Gardens, looking straight at the Gap of Dunloe, is a magnificently placed retreat.

The castle at Dunloe has a confused and disputed origin. It may have been built in 1213 by the MacThomas clan, but it is also reputed to have been built by O'Sullivan Mór. Then again, another source claims it as a Norman keep built by Meyler de Bermingham. Whatever the facts, the garden is built on what is clearly a favourable site, overlooking and commanding passages across two rivers, the Laune and the Loe.

This is not a place of framed views (apart from the Gap of Dunloe) and smart features. This garden is about the plants, and they are arranged so that the maximum

Contact: Reception
Tel: (+353) 064 664 4111
e-mail:
hotelsales@killarneyhotels.ie
www.thedunloe.com
Open: May to October, by appointment only. Supervised children welcome. Dogs on leads.
Directions: 10km from Killarney on the Killarney-Beaufort road (R562).

number of choice plants can be seen to best advantage as one walks around.

The tower house castle is set in the midst of the garden, overlooking the River Laune. A little stone path travels from here through newly planted camellia and hydrangea beds, down to a lower walk. Three-metre-high stone walls surround this area and mark the drop to the beech woods below.

Paths lead from the buildings out to the arboretum and walled garden, both filled with specimen trees and flowering shrubs. The southwest's most famous trees, the strawberry tree or *Arbutus unedo* and myrtles, grow here in great numbers. Myrtle or *Luma apiculata* comes from Chile, but does so well in Kerry that it might as well be a native.

There is far too much in this large garden to take in on a single visit and for many the handy 'Around the World in Thirty Minutes' leaflet, which marks out thirty of the most remarkable trees, will be a lifeline from the sheer mind-boggling spectacle of so many wonderful plants.

Glanleam House and Garden Valentia Island

Glanleam, like Derreen and Derrynane, is another of the great 'wild' gardens of Kerry. It was the creation of Peter Fitzgerald, the nineteenth Knight of Kerry. In 1830 he took the bare rock of Valentia Island and began to mould it into a garden. He used his many connections to fill the new garden with rare and unusual plants, many of which are still here today.

The ornamental garden is long and narrow, made up of walks through sheltering and lightly shading trees, with occasional openings and clearings. Close to the house there are lawns and a semicircular walled kitchen garden full of vegetables grown organically and ornamentally. There are also acres of exotic woods to explore.

The upper walk is the home of the camellia collection. They start flowering at the end of November

Contact: Meta Kreissig
Tel: (+353) 066 947 6176
e-mail: mail@glanleam.com
Open: Easter to October, daily 11am-7pm by appointment. Supervised children welcome. Dogs on leads.
Special features: Self-catering houses. Catered accommodation and meals can be booked.
Directions: Driving from Portmagee over the bridge to Valentia Island, follow the signs to Knightstown. In the village, turn left after the Church of Ireland. Travel along for a short distance. Glanleam is on the right, signposted.

and, like a tag team, continue in succession right through to summer. Other trails along restored Victorian pebble paths lead past a series of unusual small gardens and rare trees from all over the world.

A fern walk overhung with fringed acacias leads onto another walk of dierama, or angel's fishing rod. In the spring this site fills with bluebells and libertia. To the front of the house, walk along the gunnera walk past more naturalised tree ferns and a thundering stream to the organic kitchen garden.

The Kreissigs are dedicated to cultivating and expanding the garden: more than 22,000 oak were planted in the early 1990s, along with 15,000 ash. Restoration and planting continues.

Muckross Gardens | Muckross House, Killarney National Park, Killarney

Set among the woods and lakes of Killarney, Muckross is a truly lovely garden.

The Tudor-style house was built in 1843 for Henry Arthur Herbert.

Tel: (+353) 064 667 0144
e-mail:
killarneynationalpark@opw.ie
www.muckross-house.ie
Open: All year daily 9am-5.30pm /
July to August 9am-7pm.Closed
one week at Christmas. No entrance
fee to park and garden. Supervised
children welcome. Dogs on leads.
Special features: Partially
wheelchair accessible. Exhibition.
Craft shop. Restaurant. Self-
guiding trails, including a special
trail for the visually impaired.
Access to the restored greenhouse
by appointment to groups only.
Traditional farm, with Kerry cow
herd.
Directions: Situated 6km from
Killarney on the N71 to Kenmare.

It transferred to the Guinness family and then to the family of Senator Vincent Arthur, who presented it to the State in 1932. It stands deep in the park, surrounded by smart lawns that run smoothly down towards the famous lakes. Clipped hedges and topiary cones add a dash of formality and tidiness to these front and side lawns. Old shrub roses butt up against the building, along with an ancient wisteria. From the terrace there are views over the lakes to the mountains beyond and the beginnings of the

arboretum, with groves of sculptural Scots pine, to the foreground.

A sunken garden to the back of the house contains beds of cannas, dahlias, roses, clematis and other herbaceous plants.

A set of steps out of the sunken garden leads into the rockery, one of the great features in Muckross.

Through shrubs and rocky outcrops deep within the rockery, one catches constant glimpses of the manicured parkland in one direction and the arboretum beyond.

But before heading out to the far reaches of the woods and tree collections, the walled garden is worth a visit.

Continuing out past this and the shrub-studded lawns, there are walks through the water garden. This is a particularly attractive part of the garden, in contrast to the manicured walled and flower gardens. The paths trail alongside sunken stone-edged streams, sprouting ferns and moss and there are big clumps of crinum lilies and hostas growing by the water.

The arboretum melts off into the greater woods leading to the Torc waterfall. This is not a day's visit but a whole weekend's worth.

Ballynacourty
Ballysteen

orty-two years ago, Ballynacourty was 'a plain, unadorned old farmhouse'. Today, the handsome garden has the appearance of a place that never knew a plain or unadorned day in its life. The years

Contact: George and Michelina Stacpoole
Tel: (+353) 061 393 626
e-mail: stacpoole@iol.ie
Open: May to September by appointment to groups only. Supervised children welcome.
Directions: Driving from Limerick to Foynes on the N69, turn right for Pallaskenry. In Pallaskenry village, turn left in the direction of Ballysteen. The garden is 3km along this road on the right-hand side. The gateway is marked by pillars topped with stone urns.

since moving to Ballynacourty have been well spent by the Stacpooles. They have turned the grounds into a sophisticated, handsome garden. The references to historic landscaping are strong: the lines of hedging are architectural and mostly green.

The house is draped voluptuously with a massive wisteria. Just visible under its trailing branches is a loggia-cum-conservatory; and it all feels as much Lombardy as Limerick.

A walk through the garden starts when you make your way through an arch in a big hornbeam hedge that runs out from the house.

From this point, at the end of the privet hedge the garden meanders in several directions. One route takes in a lavender walk that leads towards a wildflower area with grass paths cut through the buttercups, cowslips and meadowsweet. An arbour of privet stands perched on a bank overlooking a sea of daffodils and the River Shannon, which flows below the garden.

Ballynacourty is an easy garden to get lost in. Only at the top of a hill overlooking the garden can the shape and plan of the place, with its feature gates, pillars, statues and hedge walls, be seen in context.

The Stacpooles also derive as much use from the natural features the land threw up as those brought in and built: old wells and huge natural stone outcrops peeping out of the well-kept lawns are used like stepping stones across a green lake.

Boyce Gardens
Mountrenchard, Foynes

The Boyces have been working this one-acre garden since 1983, and it has the look of a place on the receiving end of much love and dedication.

Contact: Phyl and Dick Boyce
Tel: (+353) 069 65 302
e-mail: dboyce.ias@eircom.net
www.boycesgardens.com
Open: May to October, daily 10am-6pm.
Other times by appointment.
Groups welcome. Not suitable for children.
Special features: Partially wheelchair accessible.
Directions: The garden is 1km from Loughill, travelling toward Glin, off the N69. Signposted.

The garden is a maze of complicated garden rooms in different styles. Arched tunnels under blankets of climbers lead from one compartment to another. The look changes constantly, morphing from a perfect little alpine garden facing south and baking in the sun, to long double borders with delphiniums, phlox, irises and other blue flowers on one side of a path and yellow ligularia and rudbeckia, solidago and on the other.

Phyl is a keen produce-grower and her tidy raised-bed vegetable garden to the rear of the garden shows what can be achieved in a compact space.

The greenhouse is set in the middle of the garden but is not visible until one almost bumps into it, so abundant are the distractions around it. It is a small structure but it is like a treasure trove, full of grapes, succulents, and a jam of other exotics.

At the lower end of the garden there is a boggy area with, among other things, a Japanese pagoda tree or sophora with zigzagging branches and miniscule sweet flowers. The garden is stuffed to capacity with plants.

Knockpatrick Gardens
Knockpatrick, Foynes

The garden at Knockpatrick, started by the O'Brien family, has been in existence for over seventy years. Since then, three generations of Tim's family have worked and developed the plot, which enjoys an enviable situation overlooking the Shannon Estuary.

Contact: Tim and Helen O'Brien
Tel: (+353) 069 65 256 /
087 948 5651
e-mail: hob68@eircom.net
Open: May to October by appointment only. Charity day in May, contact for annual dates. Supervised children welcome.
Special features: Plants for sale on charity days.
Directions: Take the N69 from Limerick for 34.5km. About 1.5km before Foynes village follow the sign for Knockpatrick. The garden is 1.5km from the cross and marked by an arched entrance.

From the gateway, you are led enticingly under an arch of dripping gold laburnum, up a drive being slowly encroached upon by magnolias, liriodendrons and peeling barked Japanese acers.

The drive runs below and parallel to the steep rock garden on top of which stands the house. This is a busy, plant-stuffed garden created using layers from ground to sky. Husband-and-wife team Tim and Helen are responsible for the extravagant show that today covers three acres.

Under their care this has become a truly varied garden, divided into different levels by pools and water features, streams and stone features like the moon gate. This pretty circular gateway both joins and separates different garden rooms. A new developing arboretum is the most recently created garden.

The whitewashed yard is a bright sun-trap and they take full advantage of the warmth it holds by growing tender echiums, shrubs like Ribes speciosum, antinidia and a whole range of different abutilons against its gleaming white walls. With the knobbly undulating lime-washed stone, gleaming bright in the sun with such a range of exotics against it, one could be forgiven for thinking they had been transported to some Greek island.

For all the new plants, the busiest and best time of the year in the O'Briens' garden is late May when most of the rhododendrons and azaleas bloom and they hold an annual charity day. Plants are potted up and teas and cakes are prepared for the crowds that arrive to enjoy the fleeting flowers and party atmosphere. Helen laughed at the thought of the crazy amount of work that goes into that open day: 'Every year we say this is the last year, and every year we do it all over again!' Such is the power of the gardening bug.

Terra Nova Garden
Dromin, Athlacca, Kilmallock

Terra Nova is a strange and wonderful garden. No matter how often I visit, it always feels like it has been given a complete overhaul since my last visit. It is a small garden, covering half an acre, yet it is almost impossible to describe how many plants in such wonderful combinations that Deborah and Martin Begley manage to shoe-horn into their garden. The Begleys are fanatical gardeners and a walk through Terra Nova almost brings on a bout of sensory overload.

Martin is the hard landscaping chief, maker of features like the little bridged frog pond, edged with canna lilies, golden gardener's garters and bulrushes. His most recent large scale addition has been the Thai house, surrounded by big tree ferns – including a *Dicksonia squarrosa*. Deborah is the plant expert, responsible for the huge

Contact: Deborah and Martin Begley
Tel: (+353) 063 90 744 / 086 065 8807
e-mail: terranovaplants@eircom.net
www.terranovaplants.com
Open: May to September by appointment only. Groups welcome. Not suitable for children.
Special features: Plants for sale. Self service tearoom.
Directions: Travel to Bruff and leave by the Kilmallock Road (R512), follow it for just over 2km. Turn right at the crossroads and follow signs for Martin Begley Glass.

number of unusual and rare plants this small garden homes so impressively.

This is a truly inspiring garden, well worth visiting, a testament to what flair, passion and back-breaking work can achieve.

Killurney
Ballypatrick, Clonmel

Driving through the gates at Killurney, looking up the drive and through peep holes under the trees and between shrubs, it is clear that this is a garden worked by an assured talent. Everything spells expertise and flair. The source of that flair is Mildred Stokes, and this has been her domain for over a quarter of a century.

Contact: Mildred Stokes
Tel: (+353) 052 613 3155 / 087 944 4662
e-mail: rowswork@eircom.net
Open: For selected open days in June. Contact for annual dates. By appointment at other times.
Special features: Partially wheelchair accessible. Teas can be arranged.
Directions: Driving from Kilkenny on the N76 turn right at Ormonde Stores. Take the third right at a sign for Killurney. Turn at the first turn on the left after the school and the house is first on the left.

The garden was designed so that, standing at the front door, two generous flanks of shrubs, trees and flowers act like huge theatre curtains, framing a view of the Comeragh mountains in the distance, over the fields that sweep down in front of the garden.

The idea of harnessing a natural sunken stream that ran along the boundary of the garden was an inspired one. Water was brought into the centre of the plot so that it could be directed to wander

along between the vegetation and bridged with flat stone slabs. It looks completely natural.

A feeling of privacy and intimacy is achieved by the strategic placement of taller plants, which then have to be skirted around in order to see more of the garden. The effect of this is to entice the visitor on to further investigation.

A classic country garden.

Cappoquin House
Cappoquin

Cappoquin House is a fine Georgian house built on the site of, and incorporating, the walls of one of the FitzGeralds' Norman castles on the River Blackwater in west Waterford.

Contact: Charles Keane
Tel: (+353) 058 54 290
e-mail:
charleskeane@cappoquinestate.com
www.cappoquinhouseandgardens.com
Open: House: May to July, daily 9am-1pm, closed Sunday and bank holidays. Other times by appointment. See web for dates. Groups by appointment only. Garden: All year Monday to Saturday 10am-4pm. Closed Sunday and bank holidays. Gates close 4.30pm. Supervised children welcome. No Dogs allowed. Not wheelchair accessible.
Special features: Castle ruins. Tours of house.
Directions: Entering Cappoquin from the N72, turn right at the T-junction in the centre of the town. The garden is 200m along on the left, with a stone gateway.

The house has been the home of the Keane family for nearly three hundred years and the garden has the air of a place that has been tended and minded for all of that time. It is chiefly the result of the nineteenth-century inhabitants, however, with extra additions made in the 1970s.

Cappoquin is an easy, pleasing garden into which a great deal of care has been poured. Real thought has gone into stylish colour mixing, particularly with the many rhododendrons and azaleas scattered throughout the place.

One of the gardens rises high above and behind the house. This is a maze of grass paths leading through meadows between groves of rhododendrons, shrubs and specimen trees, including a rarely seen specimen of *Grisselinia litoralis* grown as a tree and a huge Turkey oak or *Quercus cerris* with a girth of three-and-half-metres. From up here, Lismore Castle can be spotted in the distance.

Another route leads past a little rose garden, sheltered under an ancient-looking withholding wall. At one end of the wall, a little stream emerges from underground, creating the conditions needed for a damp garden of big ligularia and gunnera. Close by, set in between some other shrubs, a healthy little olive tree shows just how sheltered some of the planting pockets here are.

To the front of the house there is a beech hedge-enclosed garden. This is a mix of lawns, raised beds full of lambs' ears, perennial wallflower, wild strawberries and pink osteospermum twining through black grass. It is an intimate, domestic spot compared to the rest of the garden. This is overlooked by the elegant old conservatory to the front of the house.

For all its individual charms, what is most memorable about Cappoquin is the creation of so many views and vistas back and forth between well-thought-out features, old ruins covered in white roses, aged stone gateways leading seemingly nowhere and little folly-like buildings under groves of trees.

Fairbrook House Gardens
Kilmeaden

Fairbrook House garden is a lock-me-in-and-throw-away-the-key type of place that took far too long to discover. This garden was built over the past sixteen years on a remarkable site by Dutch artists Clary Mastenbroek and Wout Muller.

Contact: Clary Mastenbroek
Tel: (+353) 051 384 657 /
085 813 1448
e-mail: art@fairbrook-house.com
www.fairbrook-house.com
Open: May to September by appointment. No children under twelve. No dogs.
Special features: Contemporary art gallery. Teas by arrangement. Bric-a-brac shop.
Directions: From Waterford on the N25, take the Carrick roundabout in the direction of Cork (N25). After just over 1km take the first turn to the right. There is a sign at this corner for a low bridge. The garden is a few metres along on the right. The garden name is on the gateway.

There are streams, rills and ponds at every turn, an intriguing series of waterways that were once part of an old woollen mill built in 1776 on the little River Dawn. At different times of the year the river roars along and swells to great levels, and at other times it wanders, tamely and sedately, through the garden.

Along with the water, stone work features strongly, from walls to cobbled paths and little follies. This place is a fascinating mix of history, art, horticulture and nature.

Unusually for an Irish garden, Fairbrook features a great number of topiarised shrubs. Topiary is wonderful in all its guises, and this must be one of the best topiary gardens on the island, or indeed anywhere.

Different garden rooms lead from one to another in a beautiful series of individual gardens. An arch made out of weeping mulberry bushes leads to the dye house garden. Next door is another garden room, featuring walls of blue hazy lavender around rose beds full of white Rosa 'Winchester Cathedral'.

Following your nose, you will come upon beech and hornbeam mazes, fern gardens and an all-green garden. This interesting corner is an exercise in working with only green flowers.

It is a toss-up over which is prettier between the knot garden and the bonsai garden. Throughout the place there are pieces of sculpture placed in niches, secreted around corners, in secluded spots and out in the open, to distract from and add to the picture. The exhibitions change regularly and the old buildings and planting schemes provide each piece with the perfect exhibition space. Walking about is an object lesson in placing art in a garden setting.

Lismore Castle Garden
Lismore

Lismore Castle is like something from a fairytale: on a height looking down over the river. Lismore is one of the most beautiful towns in Ireland. There has been a castle on this spectacular site since the twelfth century, with a colourful collection of past owners and inhabitants, including Sir Walter Raleigh, Robert Boyle (the father of chemistry) and Adele Astaire, sister of Fred. The romantic castle seen today is largely a nineteenth-century creation for the sixth Duke of Devonshire, into whose family the castle passed in the 1750s.

Tel: (+353) 058 54 061
e-mail:
gardens@lismorecastle.com
www.lismorecastle.com
Open: Mid-March to September, daily 11am-4.45pm. Groups by appointment at other times. Supervised children welcome. Dogs on leads.
Special features: Partially wheelchair accessible. Castle. Art gallery. Historic town. Contemporary sculpture in grounds.
Directions: Situated in the village of Lismore.

The garden around the castle is divided cleanly into two areas: the upper and lower gardens. The upper garden, built on a slope, is reached by way of a rickety stairs up through a stone riding house that was built in 1620. This is an unusual, crooked little building that runs over the drive to the castle.

The walled garden is one of the oldest continuously cultivated gardens of its type in the country, laid out in the 1600s and worked since then. As a result, some of the plants are venerable to say the least.

Hunt out the equally venerable and unusual, accordion-shaped greenhouses designed by Sir William Paxton in the nineteenth century.

The lower garden, or pleasure ground, is linked to the upper by the riding house. It is made up of informal cobble-edged gravel paths that wind around magnolia, rhododendron and azalea in a landscape that includes a famous yew walk that was laid out in the early 1700s.

In this part of the garden there are a number of important contemporary sculptures, particularly a work by British artist Antony Gormley, which is set at the very end of the yew walk; it is a ghostly, powerful piece placed in a perfectly atmospheric spot. The use of contemporary art at Lismore adds an additional layer of variety to the garden. It shows a place with a future as well as a past to enjoy.

Mount Congreve
Kilmeaden

Mount Congreve is an astounding place, built on a scale completely different to that of any other garden on the island. It is a place that speaks of another age.

Contact: Michael White
Tel: (+353) 051 384 115
e-mail: info@mountcongreve.com
www.mountcongreve.com
Open: April to September, Thursday 9am-4.30pm. At other times by appointment. Children under twelve not admitted.
Directions: Travel from Waterford on the N25 heading towards Cork. Pass the Holy Cross pub on the right and at the next crossroads turn right. Go through one crossroads and turn left at the next crossroads. Travel for about 500m and the gates are on the right side. Follow the signs for the Estate Office.

Boasting one of the biggest collections of rhododendrons in the world, and certainly the biggest in Europe, Mount Congreve is a place of superlatives. This is the world's largest plant collection, assembled in the last half of the twentieth century and started by Ambrose Congreve a man of considerable wealth who decided, at the age of eleven, to begin planting and never stopped until his death in 2011.

There are four sloped acres of walled garden, filled with usual and a lot of unusual herbaceous plants, including special iris beds and great

runs of hydrangea in north-facing beds, as well as double borders of peony, nepeta and roses bisecting the garden.

Wander through the extensive greenhouses past walls of nectarines, a mind-bending display of orchids and bromeliads, rare fuchsias and almost extinct varieties of cyclamen and clivia.

The main body of the garden is woodland and its beauties are the flowering shrubs, runs of magnolia and camellia, rhododendron and azalea, cherry, acer, azara, eucryphia, michelia, pittosporum and prunus.

There are over sixteen miles of paths wandering in and around the plants. And there are surprises: every so often the paths open onto a secret garden, a beech lawn with rolling turf planted through with spring bulbs, secluded dells and glades, a private garden room or a temple garden.

The youth of the gardens is something one must remind oneself of continually. Mount Congreve has the feel of a garden much more mature than its double-digit age.

Tourin House and Gardens
Cappoquin

One among a string of historic gardens dotted along the River Blackwater, Tourin is particularly attractive because of its interesting mix of old and new. The garden, created around the old house and an even older castle dating back to 1560, was started as it is seen today by Kristin Jameson's parents. It is made up of a series of woodland gardens, combining new and special trees with the older park trees and specimens that were here in the 1950s, when Kristin's mother arrived from Scandinavia and started to restore the gardens.

There are spring gardens made up of cherries, azaleas and camellias criss-crossed by a network of low dry stone walls. Hostas and primulas, lily-of-the valley and fox gloves take over the show later in the year.

Contact: Kristin Jameson
Tel: (+353) 058 54 405
e-mail: info@tourin-house.ie
www.tourin-house.ie
Open: May to September, Monday to Saturday 1pm-5pm. Other times by appointment. Groups by appointment only.
Special Features: Teas can be arranged. Art classes held. Events.
Directions: 5km south of Cappoquin on the scenic road to Youghal. Signposted from both Cappoquin and Lismore.

The big walled garden is divided into pretty beds, fruit gardens, vegetable beds and greenhouses full of tomatoes and cherries.

The courtyard is something of a hub. In it, a small collection of roses collected from derelict cottages around Ireland is being developed. There is a venue for garden talks and even cinema shows and the long refectory-style tables in here were all made from felled trees in the garden.

A cherry walk leads out to the river, where they planted sixty-five acres of hardwoods six years ago. The path toward the river and Tourin Quay passes the original sixteenth-century tower house that the Victorian house replaced.

Tourin is a fascinating place being utilised in so many unique ways by an enterprising family.

Connaught

Kylemore Abbey

Ardcarraig|
Oranswell, Bushypark

A rdcarraig hugs the hilly land at the southern end of Lough Corrib. It has been here since 1971, when Lorna and Harry MacMahon arrived to take over a scrubby one-acre site around their new home.

Contact: Lorna MacMahon
Tel: (+353) 091 524 336
e-mail: oranswell@eircom.net
Open: Contact for annual dates, otherwise strictly by appointment.
Directions: Situated off the N59 about 5km out of Galway. Take second left turn after Glenloe Abbey Hotel. The garden is 250m up the road on the left, with a limestone entrance.

They took its humps and hollows and transformed them into one of the most innovative and beautiful private gardens on the island.

Following the contours of the land, the site is divided into separate garden rooms, each distinctive and linked by rising, falling and snaking paths.

The first of the different garden rooms is a dry gravel garden, made up of low-growing heathers, tall grasses and evergreen shrubs such as *Chamaecyparis filifera*, with long, string-like leaves.

From here, the garden quickly morphs into the hot stuff border, an exuberant flourish of kniphofia,

plum-coloured opium poppies or
Papaver somniferum, agapanthus,
erigeron and South African plants
that include watsonia and wine-
coloured hemerocallis.

The path runs past a chamaecyparis
being scrambled over by a big Rosa
'Albertine', between layered shrubs
and trees that gradually grow into a
dark wooded canopy. Making its way
through this, the trail emerges into the pond garden.

The path continues into the fern garden, a dark, wet spot, and from
there out to a sunny opening full of prehistoric-looking restios and a
weeping *Fitzroya cupressoides*, an unusual tree to see in Ireland.

'The whole idea here is to go from light to shade and back out into the
light again,' explains Lorna. At this point the trail reaches a little stream
that runs into the moss garden. Moss is a natural phenomenon which
looks so beautiful that Lorna rightly wonders why so many people try to
get rid of it, rather than encouraging it.

Next, we arrive at the stone lantern garden, inspired by the Japanese
style, uninterrupted by flower. A small stone bridge links this with
'Harry's garden', which Lorna made in the late 1990s as a memorial to
her late husband.

Climbing up and down the formidable hills over which the garden
is draped, on narrow little paths, the fact that Lorna, a tiny woman,
manages to cart and carry, hump and tote plants, tools and wheelbarrows
around the place, only makes it more impressive. Anyone else would want
a staff of at least four.

Cashel House |
Cashel, Connemara

. . . .

Seen from the drive, Cashel House looks as though it has flowers and shrubs climbing through its windows and doors. The paths are invisible behind plants, making the building appear to sit in the middle of a huge bed of flowers. This effect works from inside the building too: sitting in the conservatory, masses of white lychnis, red 'ladybird' poppies and lilies grow at eye level and a little bridged stream flows past beneath them.

These spreading borders reach out from the house towards the large mixed-shrub borders and, beyond these, a rising circle of woods.

In the vegetable garden, the number of lesser spotted crops is interesting. And, appropriately, these are hemmed-in not by the usual box, but by box-leaf euonymus, framing lines of kohlrabi, lovage, red kale, Florence

Contact: Kay and Lucy McEvilly
Tel: (+353) 095 31 001
e-mail:
info@cashel-house-hotel.com
www.cashel-house-hotel.com
Open: Contact for details.
Special features: Garden courses. Hotel.
Directions: South off the N59 between Oughterard and Clifden. Well signposted.

fennel and sorrel – all crops destined for the hotel kitchen.

Flanking the other side of the house is what looks like a dense wood. But stepping into it reveals an almost hollowed-out woodland garden, with camellias under-planted with hostas and primulas.

This is a large garden that has been cultivated for more than a hundred years, the sort of place where a sizable grove of impressive tree ferns can conceivably be lost under vegetation and lie undisturbed for decades.

Beyond the wood, there is a sunny area called Mary's garden – a special flower garden filled with delphiniums, lupins, phlox and roses, all melting together to make a picture that almost blinds the visitor as they emerge out of the dark wood. Rarely are such treats kept until last.

Kylemore Abbey
Connemara

In 1852, Mitchell Henry and his wife Margaret honeymooned in Connemara. Margaret fell so deeply in love with the region that her new husband bought 9,000 acres and built her a castle there. Henry imposed an impressive demesne on the rough land, employing hundreds of workers to realise his vision by 1871. But Margaret only lived to enjoy her extravagant gift until 1875 when she died. At the outbreak of World War I, the Irish Benedictine nuns fled war-torn Belgium, moving to Ireland, where they bought Kylemore and opened a girls school.

In the decades since, the extensive gardens fell into disrepair due to loss of manpower and money. But the nuns set out to restore the gardens in 1996 and today it is perhaps as handsome as when it was created.

Contact: Reception
Tel: (+353) 095 52000
e-mail: info@kylemoreabbey.ie
www.kylemoreabbey.com
Open: Grounds, daily all year 10am-5pm. Garden, mid-March to October. See web for annual dates.
Special features: Partially wheelchair accessible. Restaurant. Tea rooms. Gift shops. Castle.
Directions: On the Leenane to Clifden road (N59), 9k from Leenane.

The first section of walled garden is an unusual feature and one rarely seen. This is an example of Victorian formal bedding where annuals are grown in massive numbers to create borders that look rather like geometric floral carpets.

Two of the original twenty greenhouses have been restored and house tender plants, not to mention cats asleep on the electric propagation heat mats.

Three other features worth investigating are the restored gardener's house, a tool shed and the bothy. The gardener's house is a reproduction of the house the head gardener lived in, complete with its own little flower garden.

The bothy, on the other hand, was home to the garden boys – who had to sleep close to the boilers they had to stoke twenty-four hours a day to keep the glasshouses constantly warm. And as for the tool shed, horticultural anoraks will always enjoy a display of old and obscure implements.

Alongside the walled gardens there are extensive woodland walks through oak, lime and beech, Sitka spruce, alder, native wych elm (*Ulmus glabra*) and Monterey pine.

Portumna Castle Gardens |
Portumna

Richard Burke, 4th Earl of Clanricarde, began to build Portumna Castle and its gardens in 1618 on an impressive site overlooking Lough Derg, bordering Galway and Tipperary. The castle is one of the finest surviving examples of an Irish semi-fortified house of this period. The grounds are thought to have been laid out in the most modern and fashionable style of the time, as his wife had come from the court of Elizabeth and as a result was au fait with court fashions.

The gardens are divided into two distinctive areas. The first is a re-creation of a formal Jacobean garden laid out to the front of the castle. It is a smart, substantial array of well proportioned paths and geometric beds of roses. The house itself towers impressively over it all and standing on its steps, though it takes the house out of the picture,

Contact: Reception or Ruth Carty
Tel: (+353) 0909 741 658 / 741 625
e-mail: portumnacastle@opw.ie
Open: April to October 10am-6pm daily.
Group tours can be arranged.
Supervised children welcome.
Dogs on leads.
Special features: Working kitchen garden. Castle. Craft gardening courses.
Directions: Situated in Portumna Castle Park on the edge of Portumna town. Follow the signs from Abbey Street.

is the best way to overlook this gorgeous garden.

The second area is a walled kitchen garden. Walking into it is like entering into the middle of a riot after having just attended a deportment class. The explosion of foliage, flower, colour and sheer variety is a joy.

Neglected for over a hundred years, restoration on the kitchen garden began back in 1996 under the care of a number of local organic enthusiasts. The aim was to produce, as much as possible, an authentic seventeenth-century kitchen garden and so period techniques and plants were used to a large degree. Archaeological research led to the discovery of ancient seed in the soil, and the Irish Seed Savers Association helped to source heritage seeds using that information. Meanwhile, many of the old paths, including a turning circle for a pony and cart, were uncovered and restored.

Today, following years of development, the kitchen garden is a delight - full of vegetables, fruit grown in little orchard areas, billowing herbaceous borders and arbours draped in sweet jasmine, roses and honeysuckle. Even on days when there are plenty of visitors around, the seclusion of each little part of the walled garden means that a visitor always feels as though they have the place to themselves. I adore this beautiful garden and its happy tangle of plants.

Turlough Park Museum of Country Life | Turlough, Castlebar

The first sight at Turlough Park is of an immaculately tended grand Victorian garden. The big house stands ahead, overlooking a long run of perfect, rolled and striped lawn and well maintained paths. There are smart island beds, full of bedding plants, cut into the lawn at regular intervals with all the attendant in-your-face colours we associate with old-fashioned Victorian municipal-style beds.

Overlooking these flower beds is a fine sized greenhouse, stuffed to capacity with a range of tender plants arranged beautifully on staging. Unlike many of the better greenhouses around the country, this one is open to visitors without having to seek special permission and advance booking. The well maintained feature stands in front of some majestically tall sweet chestnut, oak and ash.

Contact: The manager
Tel: (+353) 094 903 1755
e-mail: tpark@museum.ie
Open: Tuesday to Saturday 10am-5pm / Sunday 2pm-5pm
Special Features: Museum of country life. Galleries. Cafe. Shop.
Directions: Take the N5 out of Castlebar for about 6 km. Follow the signs for Horkins. At Horkins, take the left turn and the museum is a little way down that road on the left. Signposted.

Walking in the direction of the house and museum, one path leads under a trellised arch into a completely concealed garden room. This enclosure is home to a flamboyant flower garden. Two mirroring borders full of all the usual herbaceous perennials run the length of the long rectangular space. There are lupins, monarda, acanthus, phlox, salvias and a host of other great border plants.

The lake takes up the other side of the grounds, led to by steeply terraced lawns. Beyond these there are views of the lake, a round tower in the distance and forty acres of wooded walks to explore. The garden is yet another that was lucky enough to receive help from the Great Gardens of Ireland Restoration Scheme, the European Development Fund and Bord Fáilte, while the house has become home to the Irish Museum of Country Life. Money well spent.

Strokestown House |
Strokestown

Strokestown House is an intriguing place that conjures up images of feast and famine. Once at the heart of some of the most dreadful suffering experienced during the Great Famine of the 1840s, today the

Contact: Head gardener
Tel: (+353) 071 963 3013
e-mail: info@strokestownpark.ie
www.strokestownpark.ie
Open: March to October. Check website for seasonal times.
Special features: Wheelchair accessible. Museum.
Plants for sale. Restaurant. Accommodation.
Directions: Situated in the middle of the village of Strokestown on the N5.

outhouses and stable blocks – once known as 'equine cathedrals' – provide the venue for the country's most comprehensive Famine museum.

The walled garden can be dated to the 1740s, when it was used to grow fruit and vegetables. In 1890 it was converted into a fine pleasure garden. But by around 1940, lack of manpower and money led to the almost complete loss of its once impeccable croquet lawns, rose beds and ponds.

In 1980 however, a huge restoration project was carried out

on the four-acre walled garden and the matured results can be seen today.

The walled garden is entered through an ornamental gate, made in 1914, with the words 'EK Harmon' worked into the lacy ironwork. This was a gift to Olive Pakenham-Mahon from her fiance, Edward Stafford-King-Harmon, who would die in the trenches shortly after their marriage. The gate opens onto wide paths of gravel, lined with yews backed by beech hedges and leading down to a formal lily pond.

The south-facing herbaceous border is the biggest in Ireland and Britain, according to the Guinness Book of World Records, and is based on the original 1890s border. It is a spectacular bed.

The summerhouse in the centre of the walled garden was copied faithfully from an old photograph of Olive Pakenham-Mahon as a small girl, sitting outside the original with her nanny. On the lawn, the old croquet hoops stand about, conjuring up a picture of genteel, turn-of-the-century summer garden parties.

The rose garden is made up of new hybrid teas, old roses climbing over obelisks and hanging in swags on ropes.

A gateway in the wall leads into the slip garden, where restoration work on the old glasshouses has now been completed. These had been in ruins since the 1930s; they needed a considerable amount of work and thankfully received it. Today, big runs of agapanthus grow outside, while inside there are vines and peaches. The substantial vegetable garden rounds off the garden and a collection of old garden tools will be of interest to many gardeners. The final feature is an unusual Georgian teahouse, the first-floor tearoom of which is reached by an outside staircase.

Lissadell |
Ballinfull

. . . .

Lissadell House is a strange, slightly forbidding, blocky house that feels like it must be overrun with ghosts. Overlooking the water and an expanse of lawn, there is no trace of fluff and flower around it.

Contact: Isobel Cassidy
Tel: (+353) 071 916 3150
e-mail: info@lissadellhouse.com
www.lissadellhouse.com
Open: On a restricted basis. Contact for annual details.
Special features: Museum. Exhibition gallery. Café. Plants and produce for sale. Potato collection.
Directions: Drive 7km north from Sligo on the N15 (Bundoran Road). Go through the village of Carney and turn left at the sign for Lissadell.

For these, visit the walled kitchen garden and then, for a real fix, the alpine yard. The kitchen garden is surrounded by expansive yards and multiple ranges of greenhouses. Meanwhile, inside the walls, the decorous vegetable beds are, like the whole estate, worked organically. The two-and-a-half acres are divided by cross-paths and mature espaliered apple trees. They grow a broad range of vegetables, many of which are then sold to local restaurants and sold from the courtyard shop when the garden is open.

The star of the walled garden, however, is the potato collection. It comprises over 180 varieties, grown along two of the walls. The collection runs chronologically, starting with varieties bred in 1798 and working up to the modern Irish cultivars bred in the past few years.

The path past the ha-ha, through the wildflower meadow on the way to the alpine yard, is a feature in itself, but there are enough distractions in the alpine yard to fascinate one indefinitely. It is terraced in places to accommodate the land as it slopes down towards the sea.

Out in the wider estate, there have been so many restoration projects carried out: from the planting of 14,000 oak and Scots pine and the conservation of rare orchids to the restoration of a collection of heritage daffodils. Stone walls are being restored and rebuilt everywhere, and an old stone reservoir, filled by natural streams on the land, has even been re-activated.

It was planned that Lissadell would be open year-round as a preserved house, exhibition space and garden, providing the north west with a world-class tourist attraction. However, a dispute with Sligo County Council over rights of way has led to the family more or less closing the garden. This is a crying shame and it must be rectified. It is now only possible to see the garden on a very restricted basis. Contact Lissadell for information about how it might be visited.

Ulster

Benvarden Garden

Brocklamont House

Ballyrobert Cottage Garden and Nursery

17 Drumnamallaght Road

Glenarm Castle

Sir Thomas and Lady Dixon Park

The Ledsham Garden

Brook Hall Arboretum

Buchanan Garden

Hampstead Hall

Streeve Hill

Glenveagh Castle Gardens

Oakfield Park

Salthill

Ballywalter Park

Guincho

11 Longlands Road

Mount Stewart

Rowallane Garden

Seaforde Gardens

Ballyrobert Cottage Garden and Nusery

Benvarden Garden | Dervock, Ballymoney, BT53 6NN

The estate on the banks of the River Bush had a colourful start. In the 1760s it belonged to a notorious man called John McNaughton, known in local history as 'Half-Hanged' McNaughton. A Trinity student,

Contact: Mr and Mrs
Hugh Montgomery
Tel: +44 (0) 28 207 41331
Open: May, by appointment. June
to August, Tuesday to Sunday
and bank holidays 11am-5pm.
Groups should book. Children
should be supervised. No dogs.
Special features: Farm implement
museum. Plants for sale.
Directions: From the main
Belfast-Coleraine road, take the
B62 ring road to Portrush. At
Ballybogey turn right on to the
B67. Drive 2.5km. Just before
the bridge over the River Bush
turn right. The garden is marked
by iron gates.

he eloped with a fifteen-year-old heiress, Ann Knox, whom he then killed by mistake. Because of a botched execution, he was twice hanged for his crime.

Benvarden's walled garden is one of the oldest continuously cultivated gardens on the island: the two-and-a-quarter-acre feature appears on a 1788 map drawn up by James Williamson of Dublin. Over 220 years later, it still is being worked and is a model of its type.

You enter by way of the vegetable garden, which is unusually surrounded by a fairly low wall topped with railings, so it feels quite open and airy. A greenhouse full of tender plants doubles as the ticket shop and all around it there are neat crops and plants raised in the garden for sale.

The ornamental walled garden is the main attraction. In here, the first sights that stand out are the unusual double rows of box hedging around the herb borders and flowerbeds. The outer hedges, which are clipped higher, enclose lower inner hedges like green subsets. All around the tall brick walls are deep herbaceous borders crammed with delphinium spires, spiky irises and clouds of blue and pink campanula. I love the radiating rose garden. If it was a bicycle wheel, the beds would form the triangles between the spokes and the paths would make up the knobbly stone spokes, all converging on a central fish pond and small fountain.

Leaving the walled garden by a little gate in the wall, you find yourself out in the pleasure grounds. These include a grass path walk down through yew, copper beech, pine, rhododendron and willow. It leads to a woodland pond festooned with ferns, primulas and other moisture-loving plants. This is a peaceful, quiet place made up of glittery water, dappled light and wildlife. The path then trails along towards the River Bush and an elegant iron bridge with a thirty-metre span. This was built in 1878, a testament to splendid Victorian engineering and design.

Brocklamont House | 2 Old Galgorm Road, Ballymena

The house on Old Galgorm Road is a classic Victorian villa overlooking a two-and-a-half-acre garden. This is Margaret Glynn's creation. She is a talented gardener with a feel for both plants and design.

Contact: Mrs Margaret Glynn
Tel: +44 (0) 28 2564 1459
Open: May to September by appointment. Groups welcome. Children must be supervised. Dogs on leads. Occasional plants for sale.
Directions: Leaving Ballymena on the A42 to Portglenone, the garden is 0.75km outside the town on the right and marked by black iron gates, opposite the Ballymena Academy.

Enter through big old gates, past a small gravel garden, carpeted with *Viola labradorica*, Corsican mint, campanula, sedums and cushions of hepatica. From here, one's attention is drawn up and off towards tall stands of trees and sloped lawns punctuated by shrub borders and flowers.

Overhead, sky-dusting pines lead the eye back upwards. These trees have been busily growing since my last visit ten years ago. As they grew, Mrs Glynn regularly pruned them to create more scope for under-storey planting.

Mrs Glynn's favourite plants are irises, hellebores and geraniums.

She grows scores of each. She also grows a breathtaking three hundred types of galanthus. Ferns are favourites too and, as well as fitting them into corners throughout the garden, she has built a fernery at the bottom of one of the slopes.

There is a giddy abundance of troughs around the house. Troughs done well are always a pleasure to see and there are so many perfect examples here, like rows of miniature gardens, filled with fun-sized alpines.

The old walled garden has been converted and part of it is now a patio and terrace garden aimed to catch every bit of available sun. On either side of the patio are two borders, herbaceous on one side and annual on the other. Someone called this the Botticelli garden – the two flower-filled expanses are simply voluptuous, with mixed poppies, cosmos, periwinkles and osteospermum elbowing for attention.

Ballyrobert Cottage Garden & Nursery

154 Ballyrobert Rd, Ballyclare, BT39 9RT

Maurice and Joy Parkinson have been working here since the early 1990s. The abundance of bloom and colour, scent and foliage, busy with butterflies and bees, is intoxicating. But as it travels out from the house, the garden becomes more native, wild and loose, until it finally meets with and melts into the rough Ballyclare landscape. This knitting of the two appears seamless and natural, but the work that produced that seemingly easy transition from cultivation to wilds was considerable.

The area in front of the house is called the field garden. The beds are chock-full of herbaceous favourites, like lupins, asters and irises, hollyhocks and violas. The individual beds are divided by colour and the most striking is the

Contact: Joy and Maurice Parkinson
Tel: +44 (0) 28 9332 2952
e-mail: maurice@ballyrobertcottagegarden.co.uk
www.ballyrobertcottagegarden.co.uk
Open: March to October daily. Sundays by appointment only. Other times by appointment. Groups welcome. Children must be supervised. Dogs on leads.
Special features: Plant nursery. Teas by arrangement.
Directions: Just under 1km from the centre of Ballyrobert village on the Ballyclare Road, opposite the golf club entrance.

'hot' bed, full of reds and wines, from plum-coloured hemerocallis and red crocosmia to chocolate cosmos.

Tucked behind the house, there is a box garden full of more old favourite flowers, a dovecote, the beautifully restored old barn and some well made examples of cobbled paths.

At the outer edge of each of these gardens, the cultivated plants begin to butt up against wilder natives to dramatic effect. In the formal garden, the fronts of the beds are edged in clipped box while the backs are marked by undulating old fieldstone walls, behind which a native wood trails off into a meadow and on out to the rough fields.

Out by the lake garden, the feel is very much more native. There are expansive wildflower meadows and the views over little stiles, beyond the boundary, are of the rushes and wild grass from which the Parkinsons wrested their garden.

17 Drumnamallaght Road
Ballymoney

Mrs Brown has been tending her small suburban garden, growing and minding some very hard-to-mind plants, since the late 1990s. The main garden to the back of the house includes a perfect small lawn surrounded by shrubs, small trees and an overstuffed lily-and-iris pond. But good as these are, they are really only the backdrop to the cabinet of curiosities that is her collection of pots, troughs and planters full of alpines and miniature plants.

Mrs Brown has a particular talent for arranging containers. I was particularly taken by a collection of small acers in pots gathered on a set of steps. The combination of differing shapes, spreads, leaf-colours and textures put together, makes one study each plant individually more than one would an isolated specimen.

Contact: Mrs Dorothy Brown
Tel: +44 (0) 28 2766 2923
www.ulstergardensscheme.org.uk
Open: April to September by appointment only. Groups preferred. Not suitable for children. No dogs.
Special features: Alpine plants for sale.
Directions: On appointment.

There are shallow pans of plants like self-contained miniature worlds in which she grows exquisite fuchsias the size of teacups and tiny willows with a 30cm spread. Elsewhere an arrangement of succulents on a series of ledges looks like a sweet-shop display.

Glenarm Castle
Glenarm

Glenarm Castle is set at the foot of one of the Glens of Antrim in one of the most stunning settings on the island. The drive around the coast along the A2 is a rare pleasure, devoid of ribbon development and glaring new houses. The peace only needs to be shared with a few stray sheep and the occasional boy racer. This drive would be reason enough to make a visit to Glenarm even if the gardens weren't there.

Dating back to the mid-eighteenth century and covering four acres, the gardens are a true tour de force. You enter via the former mushroom house, today set up to serve teas. This white-washed building, along with the gardener's cottage and a line of potting sheds, overlooks the first small walled garden, an area largely devoted to perfect vegetable beds.

Contact: Jane Jenkins
Tel: +44 (0) 28 2884 1203
e-mail: jane@glenarmcastle.com
www.glenarmcastle.com
Open: May to September, Monday to Saturday 10am-5pm. Sunday 12pm-6pm. Groups welcome. Children must be supervised. No dogs except guide dogs.
Special features: Tearoom. Gift shop. Plants for sale. Highland games. Tulip Festival. Food weekend.
Directions: Glenarm is on the A2, north of Larne. The castle is in the village. Special parking facilities for disabled drivers.

In the big garden over the wall there are still long lengths of intact greenhouse holding vines, spectacular apricots, peaches, climbers and iridescent blue plumbago.

From here the rest of the walled garden can be explored, beginning with some mixed beds of well-matched colours.

Surprises are everywhere: a mirroring double border of silvers, blues, yellows and variegated foliage shrubs lines the path to a central sundial, surrounded by a tall yew circle.

The centre of each yew section opens onto another garden room. One of these is a clever serpentine allée of beech hedging which leads on to a beech circle with a raised pond and fountain. That gives onto another short beech avenue. Every time the visitor thinks they have seen the full extent of this garden, another flourish appears from around a corner. It might be a contemporary stone-lined stream or an historic viewing mound.

In another direction, the mood loosens out with a wild flower meadow dissected by mown paths. Along with the native flowers, they grow vivid blue camassias in the grass. The mown paths can be seen best from the top of the viewing mound, as can the views beyond the walled garden, out to sea in one direction and onto parkland in the other.

In September, they celebrate the end of the growing season with a big open food weekend, when dishes prepared from the organic produce grown in the gardens are made and sold.

Glenarm is a singular garden: ambitious, clever and attractive.

Sir Thomas and Lady Dixon Park
Upper Malone Road, Belfast

The grounds and garden that make up this park were given to the city of Belfast by Lady Dixon in 1959. They were part of a demesne founded in the eighteenth century, attached to a house which is now gone. The main body of the park is made up of mature trees in rolling wood- and parkland along the banks of the River Lagan. The park is best known, however, for its rose gardens and as the home to the International Rose Trial grounds, which were set up in 1964.

The long runs and large beds of roses in the Sir Thomas and Lady Dixon Park work well and look good. I think it is the sheer scale of planting in the displays that is the key. The 130-acre park is an attractive and hilly place with great sweeps of lawn rising and falling in hills and hollows between groves of park trees.

Contact: Stephen Stockman
Tel: +44 (0) 28 9091 8768
www.belfastcity.gov.uk/parks
Open: All year during daylight. No entrance fee. Children must be supervised. Dogs on leads.
Special features: Annual Rose Festival.
Directions: Located south of the city on the Upper Malone Road, signposted.

There is a rose here for everyone, every situation and occasion. The long arched walks, dripping scented climbers and ramblers are a dream at the height of summer.

Every July the park is transformed into the buzzing home of the annual City of Belfast International Rose Trial, a huge event in the life of Northern Ireland horticulture. There are master classes in rose growing given by experts from all over, and a huge range of events, talks and walks arranged throughout the festival.

There are also extensive camellia gardens with over one hundred varieties to be seen. The yew walk is another notable feature and there are long sauntering trails through exotic trees and a smaller series of gardens around Malone House at the edge of the park.

My favourite feature is the Japanese garden. This was added to the park in the 1990s. It is a green valley dotted with acers, mature specimens of cornus, cryptomeria and picea planted between boulders.

The Ledsham Garden | 11 Sallagh Road, Cairncastle, Ballygally, Larne

The Ledshams came to this spot in Larne, with its view over the sea to Scotland, in the mid-1990s. They bought an exposed two-acre, hilly sheep field and transformed it into a stunningly good-looking jungle garden. The visit begins with an enticing climb up into and under a canopy of hoherias, between phlomis, cistus and roses. There are plants in every direction: overhead, underfoot, in front and behind and the scents are heady. This is a garden with room for all comers, native and exotic. Making it all the more remarkable is the fact that everything has been grown from seed and cuttings.

One could learn a great deal about how to make an exceptional garden from an unpromising site in this place. The once hostile hilly site now houses little treats of plants, like hepatica and gentian, in such

Contact: David and
Janet Ledsham
Tel: +44 (0) 28 2858 3003
e-mail: ledshamd@aol.com
Open: Mid-April to mid-October
by appointment. Small groups
preferred.
Special features: Unusual plants
for sale.
Directions: From the A8 turn left
onto the B148 sign posted for
Cairncastle. After 6km, leave the
road at the 'Old Dairy Cottage'
and fork left onto Sallagh Road.
The house just under 1km along,
below the road on the right.

numbers that they need to be culled to keep them in check. These need to be given the best of protection; they will not live well if the conditions are hard. Overhead, pruned-up acers and pittosporums deliver the dappled light the ground-dwellers love.

The sound of water can be heard at this point coming from a stream. Over the course of its way through the garden, it is banked into ponds three times and there are numerous little bridges to cross.

Out of the woods, in the full sun the path runs between wild-looking hilly flower borders full of irises, echiums, proteas and campanulas, planted on free-draining scree as they might be in the wild.

Farther along, the dry riverbed garden might be something of a horticultural joke, although it was no joke making it, according to David. The bleached stony look, like everything in this garden, looks as though it just happened.

Together the Ledshams have created a remarkable garden.

Brook Hall Arboretum
65 Culmore Road, Derry

In the late eighteenth century, successful Derry merchants erected a string of handsome villas along the banks of the River Foyle. Brook Hall is considered by some to be the finest of these, standing in a landscaped park with views of the river.

Contact: David Gilliland
Tel: +44 (0) 28 7135 1297
e-mail: candr@iol.ie
Open: All year by appointment only. Groups welcome. Supervised children welcome. Dogs on leads.
Directions: Take the A2 out of the city in the direction of Culmore and Greencastle. After two roundabouts, two giant anchors on the right mark the entrance.

The grounds cover thirty-five acres across a slope down to the river, and are part of a garden that dates back to 1780, although some parts of the walled garden were being cultivated in the 1600s. But it is the modern arboretum for which Brook Hall is renowned. This was started in 1929 by Commander Frank Gilliland. Today, it is worked by David Gilliland, an enthusiastic tree expert.

The collection of trees in the arboretum is extensive and the catalogued collection records over nine hundred varieties of trees and shrubs. The ideal way to approach it is to visit at different seasons to fully appreciate the trees and the huge changes they undergo through the year.

Apart from work in the arboretum, the walled garden was totally congested when Mr Gilliland started work here. In recent years he has cleared it out and has filled it with collections of camellia, magnolia and bamboo.

Brook Hall is not a garden of striped, rolled lawns and primped flower borders. Do not come hoping to see nail-scissors tidiness. Brook Hall is first and foremost a place to interest anyone who loves trees and shrubs and wants to study the rare and unusual.

Buchanan Garden | 28 Killyfaddy Road, Magherafelt, BT45 6EX

The Buchanans moved here in 1971 and started gardening immediately. By the mid-1980s they had been so busy that expansion to a plot across the road was necessary. That second garden,

Contact: Mrs Ann Buchanan
Tel: +44 (0) 28 7963 2180
Open: All year, Tuesday to Saturday. Book during the winter months. Groups welcome. Supervised children welcome.
Special features: Refreshments can be booked.
Directions: Leaving Magherafelt on the Moneymore Road, turn left opposite the petrol station and travel 1.6km. The garden is signposted.

across the road, is mostly made up of herbaceous plants. Its overall style is dictated by the plants the Buchanans wanted to grow. Yet the garden is a nicely arranged series of borders full of well tended, well matched flowering plants.

In the main garden, back on the other side of the road, an island of *Pratia pedunculata*, is like a sea of pale blue stars in the grass. This side of the garden has more shaded areas, but it also has its own 'sunset strip', with a view of the west-facing fields beyond. A path leading up to the sunset seat is blocked at several points by clumps of herbaceous plants to make the space more

interesting. There are more hellebores and wildflowers under the trees, including a spread of pyramidal and marsh orchids as well as fritillaries. And it all looks out over a field of Shetland ponies. Teasingly just out of their reach through the fence, there are drifts of scabious, borage, Shasta daisy, snake's head fritillaries and rose campion.

The barley sugar tree is one of the best trees to plant in a garden, as at certain times of year its leaves smell of barley sugar. My experience is that it is not always reliable in this respect, but when it happens it is a delight. It reliably scents up in this garden.

Hampstead Hall 140 Culmore Road, Derry, BT48 7RS

On arrival, this appears to be a decent garden, largely made up of raised mixed beds on top of newly made dry-stone walls, small formal lawns with sentries of clipped yew and Portuguese laurel planted in straight lines leading to the front door of the old house. There are some strong shrub and tree combinations with mixes of arbutus, embothrium and trachycarpus together. It is all ordered and smart and it complements the Georgian house. However, this is not the garden proper – for that, swing around the side of the house.

This is where Liam created his Japanese garden. Much of the space here is taken up by a pond, side planted by miniature trees and creeping greenery. Wisteria-covered bridges and sets of stepping stones span the pond and

Contact: Liam Greene
Tel: +44 (0) 28 7135 4807
e-mail: nora.greene@ntlworld.com
www.ulstergardensscheme.org.uk
Open: May to September by appointment and for occasional open days. Contact for annual dates.
Directions: Travelling out of the city in the direction of Culmore and Greencastle, turn left at the sign for Baron's Court. The garden is on the right marked by a stone wall and new gateposts.

the view across is it of a wooden Japanese summerhouse and some well shaped acers.

Stepping through a stone gateway, there is another garden room. This is reminiscent of a perfect, manicured, enclosed garden, which looks like it might be spotted through an open gate down a side street in the old quarter of a southern European city. Everything is clipped, preened and gorgeous.

Unusually, and for no reason I can put my finger on, for all its formality this feels like a garden that Liam has real fun with. There is a warm and relaxed atmosphere as well as an enormous amount of style.

Streeve Hill | 25 Downland Road, Limavady, BT49 0HP

S treeve is a country garden, spread out around a charming redbrick house and surrounded by wheat fields and groves of mature trees. Close to the buildings, the style is that of a formal flower garden, divided into small outdoor rooms by neat, waist-high box hedges.

Contact: June and Peter Welsh
Tel: +44 (0) 28 7776 6563
www.ulstergardensscheme.org.uk
Open: June to August by appointment. Groups welcome. Supervised children welcome. Wheelchair accessible.
Directions: Streeve is next door to Drenagh, on the Limavady to Coleraine road (A37).

One of the first pictures is a dramatic line of irises sunbathing under a sun-trapping, south-facing wall. Beyond these there are box enclosed flowerbeds with one box cone rising proud in the middle of each bed adding an extra oomph of vertical structure and formality to the colour-blocks.

Each bed holds single-colour herbaceous perennials. Pink, white, yellow and bronze are the base colours.

Warming themselves on the redbrick walls of the house, there are big runs of honeysuckle, jasmine,

actinidia and old roses. These reach right up to the top of the building from feet tucked into flounces of lavender and pineapple sage at the base of the wall. Further along the path is a small rose garden with obelisks and arches for the roses to climb through.

The path continues on to the kitchen garden, where a good deal of imagination went into creating cropping walls of step-over apples and artichokes.

Away from the house, the structure of the garden shakes loose into wildflower meadows with mown grass paths. They lead out to the cut-flower garden under a grove of mature maple, cornus, camellia and a number of different hollies.

With one final flourish, Mrs Welsh adds to the borrowed landscape, which in this case is made up of waving wheat fields, by planting roses like 'Wedding Day' in swags along the boundary wire fence.

Glenveagh Castle Gardens |
Churchill, Letterkenny

The nineteenth-century castle at Glenveagh sits in the middle of a 36,000-acre demesne of mountains, lakes and woods. It is the biggest single protected area of land in Ireland.

Contact: Sean O'Gaoithin
Tel: (+353) 074 913 7090 / 074 913 7391
e-mail: sean.ogaoithin@ahg.gov.ie
www.glenveaghnationalpark.ie
Open: March to October 10am-6pm. Last admission at 5pm. November to March 9am-5pm. Last admission at 4pm. Guided tours available. Groups welcome. Supervised children welcome.
Special features: Interpretive centre. National park. Restaurant. Castle.
Directions: Take the N56 north out of Letterkenny. Turn left on Termon onto the R251 and follow the signs for Glenveagh National Park.

Although it is not something generally associated with north Donegal in the way that it is with Kerry and west Cork, the Gulf Stream is largely responsible for the soft microclimate in Glenveagh. As a result, alpines, Chinese and Himalayan plants all thrive in the garden.

The potager, which covers one acre, is an important laboratory dedicated to Irish horticulture.

There are so many distractions, including the gardener's cottage garden, a confection of zigzagged box walls enclosing lilies, alliums, chives and marjoram. The special touch of adding a ribbon of primulas and alpine strawberries along the border is just one of many examples where the gardening team at Glenveagh always seem to deliver just that bit more.

Standing at the bottom of the sloped garden in front of the Gothic greenhouse, the whole layout should be inspected as a piece, after a session studying the close-ups. After that, take the route out through a lead urn-capped gate and along a camellia and rhododendron 'corridor'. This has the feel of a cool hallway out of an impressive reception room in a grand house.

The pleasure grounds are tropical in feel and brimming with remarkable plants.

The list of special rhododendrons in Glenveagh is a long one. It includes a variegated specimen called Rhododendron 'Mulroy's Variety' unique to the garden. But this is only one of many unique plants here. No matter what time of year you visit, the range of plants putting on their best show will be wide.

An impressive set of sixty-seven steps leads up through the woods to a Belvedere, or viewing garden, set out with large Italian terracotta pots.

The other features within easy walk of the castle are the rose garden and the Swiss walk, so named because of its apparent resemblance to Switzerland. The Belgian walk was more obviously so named as it was created by recuperating Belgian soldiers during World War I. The Italian garden is intimate, full of eighteenth-century statuary, paved with Donegal slate and planted around with rhododendron and pieris. The Tuscan garden is planted with griselinia hedging and decorated with busts of Roman emperors and their wives. Interestingly, none of these look as incongruous as one might think in wet, northern Donegal.

Oakfield Park
Raphoe

Arriving to Oakfield Park for a first visit can be something of an overwhelming experience. Take one hundred acres, insert several brand-new man-made lakes, huge walled gardens, follies, scores of acres of woods, several huge spring flower meadows, parterres and large scale formal gardens, complete with all the usual glass houses, sunken gardens, Japanese gardens, kitchen gardens, tennis courts and ponds – and you have Oakfield Park.

Sir Gerry Robinson and his wife Heather created all this in the last fourteen years. It is a remarkable achievement.

The distractions are everywhere and come in every shape. There are dizzying routes leading between pagoda gardens, secret gardens, pool gardens, white gardens and stream

Contact: Estate Manager
Tel: (+353) 074 917 3068
e-mail: gardens@oakfieldpark.com
www.oakfieldpark.com
Open: May to August, Wednesday to Sunday 10am-6pm (Closed Monday and Tuesday). Large groups by appointment.
Special features: 4km narrow gauge railway open Saturday and Sunday in summer. Picnic facilities. Toilets. Free car parking. Partially wheelchair accessible.
Directions: Take the Letterkenny to Lifford road (N14). Pass the exit for Raphoe and continue for 1.5km. Take the next right at the crossroads by the burnt out Cross Pub. Travel 1.5k to the car park which is on the left. The garden is on the right.

gardens. The kitchen garden is naturally substantial and filled with large expanses of well-tended vegetables, cold frames and trained fruit trees.

Flax was once grown widely around here and its luminous blue flowers were at one time a common sight. Today, flax flowers are rarely seen so the Robinsons have recently given a field over to the crop.

A huge area of the ground is given over to woods and, in keeping with its name and history, the Robinsons are trying to build up the collection of oaks here.

Creating views and vistas is another ongoing project. The most ambitious example of this is the

view from the house, downhill, over and beyond the pond and its little classical summerhouse, and on through an *allée* between the trees.

Eventually, you are bound to arrive at the train station, home to two trains, one diesel and one steam. The trains travel through newly planted mixed bluebell woods, past an even bigger lake than the summerhouse lake, through acres of reed beds and alongside a sham castle/viewing tower.

Salthill
Mountcharles

Salthill is a classic country garden brought back from the brink of extinction. It covers about 1.2 acres enclosed within tall walls behind a Georgian house on the edge of Donegal Bay.

Contact: Elizabeth Temple
Tel: (+353) 074 973 5387
e-mail: etemple@eircom.net
www.donegalgardens.com
Open: May to September, Monday to Thursday 2pm-6pm / May to July, Saturday 2pm-6pm.
Other times by appointment.
Special Features: Garden talks. Groups welcome.
Directions: In Mountcharles village, take the downhill road past the church. Turn right at the churchyard and continue to the T-junction. The garden is on the left.

The entrance leads through a byre and into a courtyard surrounded by old farm buildings. In it Elizabeth Temple rather unusually created a hot Mediterranean garden.

The fun of this garden is that, having accustomed oneself to the idea of the Med in chilly Ireland, we wander like Alice through a gateway to find ourselves in the completely different world of the main walled garden.

The design is very much centred on the plants. This is a plant-lovers heaven and the place is chock-full of rarely seen shrubs and perennials.

At the top of the garden, Elizabeth grows her vegetables in

high, ridged beds. These are also used in Glenveagh, and designed to making heavy retentive soil easier to work. Herbaceous borders and groves of shrubs run perpendicular to each other and grass paths allow the visitor to get right in between big drifts of daylilies, phlox and white sanguisorba. Flowers drift in all directions, including upwards and into the trees in the shape of a climbing aconitum twining through the branches of variegated azara.

This is plant-centred, intensive gardening at its best.

Ballywalter Park | Ballywalter, Newtownards, BT22 2PP

O ut on the windy Ards Peninsula, Ballywalter Park was built in the 1850s by the English architect Charles Lanyon for the Mulholland family, later the Lords Dunleath.

Contact: Mrs Sharon Graham
Tel: +44 (0) 28 4275 8264
e-mail:
enq@dunleath-estates.co.uk
www.ballywalterpark.com
Open: All year by appointment.
Groups welcome. Supervised
children welcome.
Special features: Teas by
arrangement.
Directions: Turn off the A20 at
Greyabbey. Take the B5 and turn
right at the T-junction. Continue
to the gate lodge on the right.

The greater gardens are chiefly comprised of a landscape park. In addition to the house, Lanyon also laid out a plan for the grounds and a great gardening programme was undertaken with 93,500 trees and shrubs planted in the winter of 1846. There are walks and rides past a lake through impressive rhododendrons with huge leaves and creamy yellow flowers. A series of streams cuts through the park. These gently meandering, bridged waterways were also designed as part of a naturalistic, picturesque landscape. Informal plantings of ferns, rodgersia and primula edge

the water. Leave this by way of an entrance to a formal pond garden.

The house stands unhampered and handsome on a terrace overlooking the park. Attached to it is the award-winning restored glass conservatory. Lord Dunleath is particularly proud of the restoration and describes with pleasure the painstaking operation involved in getting the details right, such as re-creating staging for plants using small sections of the original iron work.

Inside the walled garden the chief feature is a long rose walk and pergola made of red brick uprights and oak beams. Walking between the black and blue flowers on the ground and the scented roses around and over ones head is a real pleasure.

The rose walk leads up to a huge range of glasshouses, the first of which is fronted by a line of tall cardoons. There are actually seven greenhouses in the walled garden; they are all still standing, but in need of work.

Guincho | 69 Craigdarragh Road, Helen's Bay

Guincho seems like it has been here for a lot longer than just over sixty years. This is particularly true in the case of the four acres of woodland. The garden is substantial, full of variety and beautifully maintained. In 1982 it was added to the Northern Ireland register of gardens of outstanding historical importance.

Contact: Nick Burrowes, Head Gardener
Tel: +44 (0) 28 9048 6324
Open: April to September, by appointment to groups of fifteen or more only and for charity days. See local press or National Trust Garden Scheme for details. Supervised children welcome. Dogs on leads.
Directions: From the main Belfast to Bangor road (A2), take the Craigdarragh Road to Helen's Bay. The garden is 0.5km along on the left-hand side.

The greater garden is made up of huge sweeping lawns wrapped by a wide collar of woods. Guincho is a garden on the grand-scale. The woods contain and shelter long walks past hellebores, ferns and hydrangea, all under sheltering oak, pine, eucryphia, cordyline and rhododendron. These winding, mossy paths open every so often onto expanses of lawn, letting in daylight and lending the walker views across the garden to well

designed combinations of plants, like the massive silver fir beside a large plantation of gunnera or a sea of blue hydrangea.

Emerge from the wood to a cultivated area of lawns edged with myrtle and willow, with splashes of geranium, osteospermum, *Fascicularia pitcairnifolia* and cotoneaster draping over a stone wall.

In the area close to the house there are smaller, more domestic-sized garden rooms with select and unusual small trees and flowering shrubs knotted through with climbers. A series of tiny gardens come as a surprise. Some are sunken, some are circled by tall architectural walls of phormium, some by hedges. Within these little rooms there are small lily ponds marked by mop-head bays and topiary in pots.

The terraces and balconies around the house are cleverly decorated with old varieties of apples and pears trained as balcony fences and boundaries. Standing on the terrace and looking down from a height, over these and to flowering magnolias and cherries in the garden below, is an experience.

11 Longlands Road
Island Hill, Comber

The straight, smart, green lines of hedging are like the signature of this garden. They frame and enclose, divide and wrap around swathes of herbaceous plants in ways that make this a special garden.

Contact: David McMurran
Tel: +44 (0) 28 9187 2441
e-mail:
davidmcmurran@btinternet.com
www.ulstergardensscheme.org.uk
Open: For one weekend each year. Contact in spring for annual details.
Directions: Take the A21 To Newtownards from Comber and travel for aproximately 1 Km. Turn right and the house is 300m along on the right, clearly visible.

There are sharp ideas at play everywhere – such as the 'secret' gravel walk down the centre of a wide herbaceous border. From head-on, this appears to be one solid border. But a little path through it divides it in two, and the splashes of Jacob's ladder, daylilies and other self-supporting perennials can be enjoyed from different angles as one walks between them.

Rather unusually, the plants wash right up to the edges of the building and the garden seems as though it might invade the house: a bulging hosta pond placed right beside one of the windows gives the indoor onlooker more to look at

than any television could. Lights are used fairly widely through the garden so that much of it can be seen and enjoyed at night.

At the front of the house there are two long serpentine herbaceous borders, cheerfully advertising this as a must-see garden. Perfect striped lawns and well maintained box walls between these borders all display impeccable old-school upkeep.

Peeping around the outer boundary, I saw too that the urge to expand has been too strong to resist. Along the outside of the hedge, he is busy beautifying what would otherwise be a plain place, planting shade-loving, ground-covering hellebores, spring bulbs and woodland plants.

Mount Stewart | Newtownards, Portaferry Rd, Newtownards, BT22 2AD

Everything about Mount Stewart is aimed to impress: its size at ninety acres, the enormous variety within its many gardens, the care employed in its upkeep, the wit of the design and even the standard of the guided tours.

Contact: Paul Rowlinson, Head Gardener
Tel: +44 (0) 28 4278 8387 / 4278 8487
e-mail: mountstewart@nationaltrust.org.uk
www.ulstergardensscheme.org.uk
Open: March, daily 10am-4pm / April, 10am-6pm / May to September, 10am-8pm / October, 10am-6pm. Supervised children welcome. Dogs on leads.
Special features: Partially wheelchair accessible. Sensory garden trail. Tearoom. Sales of plants raised in the garden. House and garden tours. Garden fairs. Jazz concerts. Events.
Directions: Situated on the A20 between Newtownards and Portaferry.

Mount Stewart House is an impressive pile in honey-coloured stone, and somewhat unusual in that it does not stand in splendid isolation on a lawn or on a wide spread of gravel or a restrained terrace. Standing just a hundred metres from the wide steps that lead to the door, one could equally be in a jungle of the finest plants. The house has to do battle with vegetation for attention. Even the paving around it is colonised by lavender. Tall, peeling eucalyptus, elegant conifers and seas of variegated phlox, waving anemones, great Florence Court yews, cordylines, wonderful clipped bays, irises and a thousand other plants all distract from the house in every way possible.

The garden was designed by Edith, Lady Londonderry, in the 1920s, when she arrived to live in Mount Stewart, a place she declared 'damp and depressing', situated as it was between the Irish Sea and Strangford Lough on the Ards Peninsula. By the time she had finished, Mount Stewart was home to an extraordinary series of formal gardens.

The formal gardens are broken into large rooms. Between the Spanish and Italian gardens, the huge, iconic leyandii cypress hedge is cut with nail-scissors perfection into a series of arches that resemble a huge green viaduct.

More hedging surrounds Mount Stewart's most famous feature: the Shamrock garden with its huge Red Hand of Ulster picked out in red bedding, begonias and double daisies set into gravel. The hand is set off against a green topiary harp, which towers four and a half metres over it.

The most romantic of all the gardens is the Mairi garden, created for Edith's daughter, Lady Mairi. This was where she would be brought for her daily turn in the pram. A little bronze fountain incorporates a statue of the baby girl spraying water in a haphazard way that will please children more than parents, as they get squirted by the little imp.

There are wonderful statues of gryphons, turtles, crocodiles and dodos scattered throughout the Ark Garden. These are references to a long-lost political and family in-joke, but fortunately also appeal to the uninitiated.

Mount Stewart is a full day's visit, and it might even be two if you really want to study the individual gardens, and then take in the lake and woodland walks, as well as the famed Temple of the Winds overlooking the lough, reckoned by some to be the finest garden building in Ireland.

The lake walk is becoming more and more beautiful, as acers, magnolias and other fine shrubs grow ever bigger.

Rowallane Garden | Saintfield, Ballynahinch, BT24 7LH

In 1903, Hugh Armytage Moore, a man deeply interested in plants, inherited this 1861 house and garden just outside Saintfield and started growing some of his special plants in the yards and fields around the farm and went on to create the garden we know as Rowallane today – a fifty-acre spree of landscaped gardens, wild flower meadows, rhododendron plantations, woods, rock and walled gardens.

The larger garden is a natural, wild, Robinsonian-style garden that ranges over the hilly, rocky drumlins of south County Down. It is renowned for its spring displays, when vast numbers of daffodils and rhododendrons burst into flower. But it is a garden that looks wonderful twelve months of the year.

The famous Rowallane rock garden was created by relieving a

Contact: The Manager
Tel: +44 (0) 28 9751 0131
e-mail:
rowallane@nationaltrust.org.uk
Open: 17 March to October, Monday to Friday 10.30am-6pm, Weekends 12.00-6pm / November to 17 March, Monday to Friday 10.30am-5pm. Children welcome. Dogs on leads.
Special features: Walks for the visually impaired can be arranged. Home of the National Collection of penstemon. Tearoom. Gift shop. Second-hand garden book shop.
Directions: 1.5km south of Saintfield, off the A7.

huge outcrop of the local stone, called whinstone, of its soil and scrub. Pockets were then filled and planted up with meconopsis, including gentians, primulas, bulbs, erythroniums, celmisias, heathers and leptospermum.

It is in the walled gardens that many of the treasures are to be found. It covers two acres and varies between strictly clipped, box-enclosed ten-metre runs of agapanthus, even longer runs of glorious yellow *Cephalaria gigantea*, penstemon and looser beds of tumbling peony and bergenia, inula and camellia.

There are a series of lovely stone buildings scattered about the greater grounds. These house second-hand gardening bookshops, tea rooms and shelters from the rain. The wider pleasure grounds are also marked at various points by old stone walls and boundaries. One is never quite sure whether a wall or a little stone building up ahead means that the centre of the garden is ahead or if one has become hopelessly lost. I love it.

Seaforde Gardens | Seaforde, Downpatrick, BT30 8PG

The drive up to Seaforde is like driving through a mossy valley under tunnels of mature trees, between walls of ferns.

The garden dates back to the 1750s and was probably the work of the great landscape gardener, John Sutherland. It originally involved extensive woodlands, shelter belts and screens. There was also a network of winding drives, including the charming present entrance drive.

This format had descended into a wilderness of bramble and laurel until the mid-1970s, when Patrick Forde took it in hand and began to bring the garden back to a presentable state.

A maze of hornbeam was planted in 1975, which is now a large puzzle complete with an arbour and statue of Diana. The area around the maze

Contact: Charles Forde
Tel: +44 (0) 28 4481 1225
e-mail:
info@seafordegardens.com
www.seafordegardens.com
Open: April to September,
Monday to Saturday 10am-5pm,
Sunday 1pm-6pm.
Groups welcome. Guided tours can be booked.
Supervised children welcome.
Special features: Butterfly house. Tearoom. Home to the National Collection of eucryphia.
Directions: On the Belfast–Newcastle road. Look out for the signposts in the village of Seaforde.

has been formalised through the addition of new wide gravel paths.

Next to the maze, the garden proper begins with well laid-out groves of rhododendron and large shrubs, such as an incredibly tall mahonia, used to accommodate climbing roses. Huge echiums and mimosas are grand by themselves but even more diverting with melianthus and hostas planted in numbers underneath.

It is not hard to get lost, coming across a eucryphia walk in the process, with its laden-down branches of white and pink flowers, in the case of *Eucryphia lucida* 'Pink Cloud' and E. *milliganii* 'Whisper', both of which have shell-pink blooms. These are part of the National Collection of twenty-three species and hybrids.

One of the great pleasures of this garden is standing back and enjoying the sight of maturing groves of trees, shrubs and climbers, many of them rare and unknown in any other garden on the island.

There is a butterfly house to occupy non-gardeners. This tropical butterfly house is set in a huge greenhouse planted like a jungle and home to hundreds of colourful butterflies, flying freely about, settling on branches and leaves.

Glenarm Castle

Acknowledgements

First and foremost I want to thank my husband Michael, always enthusiastic and willing to back me up on every endeavour. The encouragement he, Mary Kate and Michael junior give makes what I do possible.

Thank you to my two families, particularly Mum and Dad, Mary and Billy, Dor and Michael Lanigan senior. I want to thank Jonathan Williams. As an agent going above and beyond the call of duty seems to be his standard practice.

As an editor, Daniel Bolger has the unquantifiable talent of making the hassled business of bringing out a book a pleasant and smooth experience.

I want also to thank Seán O'Keeffe, Caroline Lambe, Alice Dawson, Clara Phelan and everyone at Liberties Press. They are a professional and civilised lot.

Gerry Daly and Mary Davies of the Irish Garden have been kind and generous for years.

Lastly, I want to thank the gardeners and owners of all the gardens I have visited. Without them there would be no book.

Photograph Credits

Airfield	*Airfield*
Altamont Gardens	*Con Brogan*
Ardcarraig	*Lorna McMahon*
Ardgillan Demesne	*Istockphoto*
Ballymore Garden	*Paul Sherwood*
Ballynacourty	*Sebastian Stacpoole*
The Cottage Garden	
Plant Center	*Maurice Parkinson*
Ballywalter Park	*The Lady Dunleath*
Bantry House and Gardens	*Fáilte Ireland*
Beaulieu House and Gardens	*Beaulieu*
Bellefield House	*Paul Barber*
Belvedere House	*David Knight and Belvedere and Garden*
Benvarden Garden	*Val Montgomery*
Birr Castle Demesne	*Birr Scientific and Heritage Foundation, Istockphoto*
The National Botanic Gardens	*Con Brogan*
Buchanan Garden	*Brian Webb*
Bunratty	*Istockphoto*
Burtown House	*James Fennell*
Caher Bridge Garden	*Carl Wright*
Coolcarrigan House	*Robert Wilson-Wright*
Coolaught Gardens	*Harry Deacon*
Derreen	*David Bingham*
Dromboy	*Charlie Wilkins*
17 Drumnamallaght Road	*Shirley Lanigan and Frank Brown*
The Duignan Garden	*Carmel Duignan*
Fairbrook House Gardens	*Clary Mastenbroek*
Farmleigh	*PHP Photography*
Fota Arboretum and Garden	*David O'Regan*
Gash Gardens	Ross Doyle
Glanleam House and Garden	*Meta Kreissig*

Glebe Gardens
and Gallery *Rohan Reilly*

Glenarm Castle *Conor Tinslon*

Glenveagh Castle
Garden *Sean O'Gaoithin*

Guincho *Gail Cairns*

Hampstead Hall *Hall Brian Webb*

Heywood Garden *Con Brogan*

Hotel Dunloe Castle
Gardens Beaufort *Hotel Dunloe Castle*

Hunting Brook
Gardens *Jimi Blakes*

Ilnacullin *Cormac Foley*

Inish Beg Gardens *Paul Keane*

The Japanese
Gardens and
St. Fiachra's Garden *Irish National
Stud Co.*

June Blake's Garden *June Blake*

Kilfane Glen and
Waterfall *Richard Mosse*

Kilgraney House
Herb Garden *Martin Marley*

Kilgraney
(Main House) *Rai Uhlemann*

Killineer House
and Garden *Charles Carroll*

Killurney *Shirley Lanigan*

Kilmacurragh
Botanic Gardens *Seamus O'Brien*

Kilmokea Manor
House and Gardens *Emma Hewlett*

Kilravock Garden *Phemie Rose*

Kilruddery House
and Gardens *James Fennell*

Knockpatrick
Gardens *Tim O'Brien*

Kylemore Abbey *Gareth McCormack,
Istockphoto*

Lakemount *Harpur Garden
Images*

Lismore Castle
Garden *Lismore Castle*

Lissadell *Pamela Cassidy*

Lodge Park Walled
Garden and Steam
Museum *Patrick Ardiff*

Marlay Demesne and
Regency Walled
Garden *Dun Laoghaire
Rathdown County
Council*

Terra Nova Garden	*Martin and Deborah Begley*
Mount Congreve	*Richard Cutbill*
Muckross Gardens	*Cormac Foley*
Patthana Garden	*TJ Maher*
Phoenix Park Walled Victorian Garden	*Richard Johnston*
Portumna Castle Gardens	*Con Brogan*
Poulnacurra	*Harpur Garden Images*
Powerscourt Gardens	*Suzanne Clarke*
Primrose Hill Gardens	*Gay O'Neill*
Rowallane Garden	*Averil Milligan*
Royal Hospital Kilmainham	*Gráinne Larkin*
Salthill	*Elizabeth Temple*
Seaforde Gardens	*Charles Forde*
Boyce Gardens	*Dick Boyce*
The Dillon Garden	*Helen Dillon*
Talbot Botanic Gardens	*Istockphoto*
Tourin House and gardens	*Kristen Jameson*
Turlough Park Museum of Country Life	*Noreen Hennigan*
Woodstock Gardens and Arboretum	*Kilkenny County Council Parks Department*